Grandmothers Counsel the World

Grandmothers
Counsel the World

*Women Elders Offer Their Vision
for Our Planet*

Carol Schaefer

FOREWORD BY WINONA LADUKE

Trumpeter

BOSTON

2006

Trumpeter Books
An imprint of Shambhala Publications, Inc.
Horticultural Hall
300 Massachusetts Avenue
Boston, Massachusetts 02115
www.shambhala.com

Quotations from Bernadette Rebienot in the chapters "Women's Wisdom"
and "Our Mother Earth" originally appeared in her article, "Thirteen
Indigenous Grandmothers," in *World Pulse,* issue 2.

9 8 7 6

Printed in the United States of America

❂ This edition is printed on acid-free paper that meets the American
National Standards Institute z39.48 Standard.

♻ Shambhala Publications makes every effort to print on recycled paper.
For more information please visit www.shambhala.com.

Distributed in the United States by Random House, Inc., and in Canada
by Random House of Canada Ltd

Interior design and composition: Greta D. Sibley & Associates

Library of Congress Cataloging-in-Publication Data

Schaefer, Carol, 1946–
Grandmothers counsel the world: wise women elders offer their vision
for our planet/Carol Schaefer.
p.   cm.
ISBN 978-1-59030-293-4 (alk. paper)
1. Earth—Folklore. 2. Women—Folklore. 3. Spirituality. I. Title.
GR655.S32 2006
398.27—DC22
2006013386

For the seventh generation and beyond

Contents

Acknowledgments   *ix*

Foreword   *xi*

Note to the Reader   *xiii*

Statement of the International Council of
Thirteen Indigenous Grandmothers   1

Introduction   3

PART ONE

The Grandmothers

Agnes Baker Pilgrim (*Oregon*)   15

Bernadette Rebienot (*Gabon, Africa*)   21

Flordemayo (*Nicaragua/New Mexico*)   27

Margaret Behan (*Montana*)   35

Rita Pitka Blumenstein (*Alaska*)   43

Tsering Dolma Gyaltong (*Tibet*)   51

Mona Polacca (*Arizona*)   55

Rita Long Visitor Holy Dance and
Beatrice Long Visitor Holy Dance (*South Dakota*)   61

Maria Alice Campos Freire (*Brazil*)   69

Clara Shinobu Iura (*Brazil*)   77

Aama Bombo (Buddhi Maya Lama) (*Nepal*)   83

Julieta Casimiro (*Mexico*)   87

Other Women Elders   93

PART TWO

Guidance for Our Times

Prophecies   115

Women's Wisdom   133

Sacred Relations   145

Our Mother Earth   161

Oppression   173

Nature's Pharmacy   189

Prayer   205

Appendix   211

Acknowledgments

WEAVING THE VOICES of the Thirteen Grandmothers, such powerful and holy women, has been an enormous privilege and has changed forever the way I see life and how I want to be in the world. I am profoundly inspired by their passion and their dedication toward helping this planet become a sacred home for humanity and all of Creation.

I am grateful to my editor, Eden Steinberg, for believing in the vision of the Grandmothers' book from the beginning, even before the council met for the first time. And I am also very appreciative of my agent Lynn Franklin's tremendous support throughout the entire process of writing the book.

The Center for Sacred Studies has my deepest gratitude, especially Jyoti, Ann Rosencranz, Carole Hart, and her late husband Bruce Hart, producers of the documentary about the Grandmothers, for providing so much information and assistance.

I am very thankful to Donna Kaye White Owl for our friendship and for our conversations that opened up worlds as I tried to fathom the beauty of indigenous ways. My gratitude goes also to another great friend, Bonnie Corso, for her insights and constant support; to Artour Toulinov for teaching me so much about photography and for always being there for me; to Bob Kirby for being the best brother anyone could wish for; and, to my father, Walker Kirby, for teaching me to love books.

I am so blessed to have the love and encouragement my three terrific sons and their great wives: Jack and Anna Ryan, Brett and Jessica Schaefer, and Kip and DeAnna Schaefer, to whom I owe a special thanks for their unconditional support. And I am especially blessed to have eight beloved grandchildren: Dylan, Mia, Asia, and Tess Ryan; Cole and Reed Schaefer; and Hudson and Quinn Schaefer. It is because of my hopes and dreams for them, for their children, and their children's children— for the future of all children—that I wrote this book.

Foreword

THE POWER OF WORDS told over generations, remembered from trees, dreams, and ancestors, is a power inherent in indigenous cultures, contained within the fabric of our way of life. The value of the oral tradition, of the teachings contained in the messages that have passed between generations, is the value of relationship. Stories and instructions shared in relationship, reaffirming relationship within a community as it joins in the social dance or song, validate and strengthen community—as do the words of these women, these *Nokomisinag,* or grandmothers.

For many years, these words have been cached away. I have had some opportunities to hear many of these women speak, and I have observed some of them as I have traveled into their communities. What I know, in the least, is that their words have immense power and connect me to a larger reality in which I, as a spiritual human being, have a place in history—they remind me that I live in both the material and spiritual worlds. That is the power of these teachings: we remember and revitalize our connections. And, from this set of relationships and teachings, we are better able to care for our communities, whether this community has feet, wings, fins, roots, or paws.

In industrial society, this kind of connection is severed. Historically, words have been written by "experts" and presented to a privileged audience, those who could read and were invited to hear those gifts to community. The words of indigenous elders have rarely been part of the discourse of "civil society"—we have instead been objectified. The experts are usually those schooled in Western teachings, scientific logic, and Judeo-Christian theology. Words come to mean less and less, it seems, the more they are written down, yet those words have been used to create a society that is unsustainable, built on conquest, blood, and land.

It is a new millennium. Most of the buffalo have been killed, many of our ancestors have been destroyed with a sword or a smallpox blanket, water is poisoned, and global climate destabilization is upon us. Within the teachings of industrial society there are few tools to address the level of catastrophic destruction we are facing. Focusing on this year's fiscal budget is not only short-term thinking, but it lacks any resonance with the natural world or with history. In short, we may believe that we are accountable to humanity's laws of trading pollution credits (trading "allowable" limits of contaminants) and paving every meadow as a "development right," but in the end, we all have to drink the water and breathe the air.

Within the wellspring of the teachings presented in this book is a path toward sustainability, what my people call *minobimaatisiiwin*, or "the good life." These teachings remind us that it is essential to reciprocate with our relatives, to be thankful, and to check our own behavior (not manage the behavior of our other relatives through such paradigms as natural resource management). After all, the accelerated extinction of species is what we have created with our hands and with our current paradigm—much extinction of the past few centuries is not a product of the natural world.

Within the words of these grandmothers are the words of real experts. There is no way to replace intergenerational knowledge of how to live sustainably, how to reaffirm relationship. The scientific paradigm, a mechanistic methodology, will not show us the way through these challenging times.

We are blessed with the teachings the Grandmothers offer, and we are thankful for their words. The range of teachings presented here from different walks of life, distinct traditional cultures, offers an amazing orchestra of knowledge. Their collective power, in voice and in presence, is profoundly impressive. *Miigwech Nokomisinag, miigwech*. (Thank you, Grandmothers, thank you.)

—*Winona LaDuke*

Note to the Reader

IT HAS BEEN A GREAT HONOR to work closely with the International Council of Thirteen Indigenous Grandmothers in crafting this book. It has been humbling for me to note that the sum total of all the years of life lived by the Grandmothers adds up to 859. Furthermore, the cultures they represent have histories that span millennia.

There is no way that any one writer, any one individual, can become a voice for the collective wisdom of the ages. I have done my best to express what I have heard and learned from the Grandmothers, but my ability to act as a bridge or translator to a wider audience is, to a certain extent, hindered by the limits of my own understanding and experience. I assume full responsibility for any misrepresentations or failures to rightfully express the teachings and mission of the Grandmothers Council.

Finally, though my name appears on the cover of this book, the words of wisdom expressed within it are not mine, and I do not lay claim to them. In a sense, this book represents our collective spiritual heritage.

May the words of the Grandmothers spread love, faith, hope, and charity for all who come upon them.

—*Carol Schaefer*

Grandmothers Counsel the World

Statement of the International Council of Thirteen Indigenous Grandmothers

WE ARE THIRTEEN INDIGENOUS GRANDMOTHERS who came together for the first time from October 11 through October 17, 2004, in Phoenicia, New York. We gathered from the four directions in the land of the people of the Iroquois Confederacy. We came here from the Amazon rain forest, the Arctic Circle of North America, the great forests of the American Northwest, the vast plains of North America, the highlands of Central America, the Black Hills of South Dakota, the mountains of Oaxaca, the desert of the American Southwest, the mountains of Tibet, and the rain forest of central Africa.

Affirming our relations with traditional medicine peoples and communities throughout the world, we have been brought together by a common vision to form a new global alliance.

We are the International Council of Thirteen Indigenous Grandmothers. We have united as one. Ours is an alliance of prayer, education, and healing for our Mother Earth—for all Her inhabitants, for all the children, and for the next seven generations.

We are deeply concerned with the unprecedented destruction of our Mother Earth: the contamination of our air, waters, and soil; the atrocities of war; the global scourge of poverty; the threat of nuclear weapons and waste; the prevailing culture of materialism; the epidemics that threaten the health of the Earth's peoples; the exploitation of indigenous medicines; and the destruction of indigenous ways of life.

We, the International Council of Thirteen Indigenous Grandmothers, believe that our ancestral ways of prayer, peacemaking, and healing are vitally needed today. We come together to nurture, educate, and train our children. We come together to uphold the practice of our ceremonies and affirm the right to use our plant medicines free of legal restriction. We come together to protect the lands where our peoples live and upon which our cultures depend, to safeguard the collective heritage of traditional medicines, and to defend the Earth Herself. We believe that the teachings of our ancestors will light our way through an uncertain future.

We join with all those who honor the Creator and all who work and pray for our children, for world peace, and for healing of our Mother Earth.

For all our relations:

Margaret Behan, Cheyenne/Arapaho

Rita Pitka Blumenstein, Yupik

Julieta Casimiro, Mazatec

Aama Bombo, Tamang

Flordemayo, Mayan

Maria Alice Campos Freire, Brazil

Tsering Dolma Gyaltong, Tibetan

Beatrice Long Visitor Holy Dance, Oglala Lakota

Rita Long Visitor Holy Dance, Oglala Lakota

Agnes Baker Pilgrim, Takelma Siletz

Mona Polacca, Hopi/Havasupai/Tewa

Clara Shinobu Iura, Brazil

Bernadette Rebienot, Omyèné

Introduction

IN A MAGICAL VALLEY, protected by the ancient spirits of the towering Catskill Mountains, a sacred fire was lit.

The flame that kindled the sacred fire was originally ignited in 1986, just outside the United Nations Building by Chief Shenandoah of the Iroquois Nation. He rubbed two sticks together to create a spark, then lit a torch for peace in the International Year of Peace. That morning, in the gleaming sunlight of a beautiful sunrise, the UN building shone like the envisioned "Great Hall of Mica" spoken of in Hopi prophecy for over a thousand years. A message was to be delivered at an amazing shining place at the time of the "Great Turning," in hopes of ushering in a millennium of peace in the world. The Hopi knew the times described in the prophecy had come.

Through extraordinary cooperation, the peace torch traveled from the Great Hall of Mica around the world through sixty-two countries in eighty-six days. During the flame's miraculous journey, it was borne by thousands of runners and witnessed by millions of people, including many world leaders (fulfilling the dream of David Gershon, author and expert on empowerment, and his wife, Gail Straub, to ignite a worldwide vision of peace and unity). When the torch returned to the United Nations, there were incredible stories about the powerful alchemical nature of the fire. Afterward, the flame was brought to the altar of the holy Santuario de Chimayo in New Mexico, where it has since been kept burning, except for when it traveled to the hallowed land of the Iroquois in 2004.

Surrounded by golden woods and in the cool, still, evening air of mid-October 2004, the flame initiated an unprecedented and historic gathering of thirteen indigenous Grandmothers from around the world, keepers of their tribes' teachings from original times. The Grandmothers had come to fulfill another ancient prophecy, known by many of the world's indigenous tribes: "When the Grandmothers from the four directions speak, a new time is coming."

The council, which had been spoken of in prophecy and seen in visions since time immemorial, finally emerged in the aftermath of 9/11. The Grandmothers' participation in the council had been foretold to each of them in different ways. When they were very young, a few of the Grandmothers had been told by their grandmothers that this was their destiny. All of the Grandmothers had been invited long ago, in a time before time as we know it, to meet at the time of the Great Turning to become a force for peace in the world. Prophecy revealed to each one that they must now share even their most secret and sacred ways with the very people who have been their oppressors, as the survival of humanity, if not the entire planet, is at stake.

The urgency of the world's situation requires a global response. The Grandmothers, living legends among their people, represent tribes from the Arctic Circle; North, South, and Central America; Africa; Tibet; and Nepal. As the wise women, *curanderas,* shamans, and healers of their tribes, they were bringing to the council new visions and new prophecies for humanity, their tribes' rich and varied sources of wisdom, and each tribe's unique and secret teachings for living within the Divine Order of all things.

Until recent history, in every part of the world communities of indigenous peoples functioned as if one with their particular environment. As a result, the many tribes of this earth mirrored the lands of their origins and thus revealed the great diversity inherent in humanity. The unique culture of each of the thousands of indigenous tribes evolved from their necessary participation with the animals, plants, and the climate of the land on which they lived. Traditions, rituals, stories, art, and music were created that were as specific to their place on Earth as the flowers and trees found there. This is why indigenous peoples say that if their connection to the land is gone, as has happened to most Native Americans, they are no longer who they were.

Some tribes, like the Cheyenne and Lakota, are taught that their first language was given to them by the animals and sounds of nature in their environment. This first language is still used in ceremony and ritual because according to tradition these sounds have the power to open the doorway to the Spirit World. Legends remind the tribes that all they know they learned by observing the various kingdoms of nature and that their role in return is to respect Mother Earth and be Her caretaker. Such intimacy with nature has enabled those who have remained on the land of their ancestors to live from the land and still maintain the Earth's balance for tens of thousands of years.

Basic to each tribe's survival, the Grandmothers say, was their ability not only to live in harmony with nature but with one another. The strength of the tribe was founded on family, and the well-being of each family was essential to the well-being of the community. Nature was seen as mirroring the different roles within a family. A common belief was that men and women are Spirit alive in the flesh, as evolving reflections of the love of their Creator, the mother/father principle. The Earth was seen as the Great Mother, the giver and nurturer of life, the female energy principle. The sky and the heavens most often were seen as the Father or Grandfather, the male energy principle.

Because of their absolute dependence on nature, indigenous peoples held that all of life was sacred. They did not see themselves as separate from nature or the cosmos, the Grandmothers tell us. So what was done to the Earth and the inhabitants of the Earth was also done to themselves. Everything was a part of the One. The animals and plants of Earth were never objectified. The objectification of nature opens the door for mistreatment and a lack of respect. As Joseph Campbell, in his PBS series with Bill Moyers, has pointed out, "The ego that sees things as a thou is not the same as one seeing things as an it."

In accord with the inherent authority within a family, traditionally the women elders, the grandmothers, were the ones who were looked up to as guardians to watch over the physical and spiritual survival of the family, and thus the tribe. They became the keepers of the teachings and rituals that allowed the tribe to flourish, and they upheld the social order. In many of the tribes around the world, including the great Iroquois

Nation (whose constitution inspired the United States Constitution), the Council of Grandmothers was always consulted before any major decision was made, including the decision of whether or not to go to war.

Indigenous peoples lived in a communal system that was based on reciprocity—everyone sharing what they had and everyone taking care of everyone else. There was no hoarding, thus no one in the tribe ever went without and all prospered equally. Food brought back by the hunters was for the whole tribe. If one hunter was particularly skilled or successful, there was no concept of keeping more for himself as a result. Instead, he was given a place of honor in the tribe.

Since there was no perception of scarcity, except what the whole tribe experienced, there was no need for excessive accumulation of personal holdings. The tribes knew what they needed to do to sustain themselves sufficiently. Most had learned that sharing and transferring increased the value of what was given, and accumulation beyond the point of enough actually stopped the flow of resources. When everyone benefited, the individual benefited more. Now, for most indigenous people, one step out of their community and into the modern world, and they can't eat or find shelter or live without money. One day in the modern world can wipe out thousands of years of sustainability.

We can learn from the tribal system how all of humanity can thrive today, the Grandmothers remind us. And indigenous peoples can also learn from the modern world how to sustain themselves when moving outside of their traditional communities.

Also common to indigenous peoples, the Grandmothers say, is an honoring and dependence upon the Spirit World, a world that is accessed through nature. To many indigenous peoples, even the stones have Spirit. In fact, the most ancient memories are attributed to stones, because the stones are thought to be the oldest beings on the planet. Most indigenous teachings hold that it is in the heart of a thing that its spirit can be found, and within that spirit is the very essence of the Creator, or whatever one wants to call this divine force. It is believed that the simple act of picking up a stone and holding it in silence changes a person in subtle and profound ways. Finding worlds within a simple stone reveals worlds within oneself, the Grandmothers tell us. Having the courage to look within and without was an important attribute in most indigenous cultures. In fact, having such close contact with nature made such an inner journey almost unavoidable.

Visions, dreams, prayer, ceremony, and ritual are the means to access the sacred Spirit World through nature, the Grandmothers tell us. Ceremony and ritual allow participation in the myths or archetypes of the culture and serve to take one out of ordinary reality. Rituals powered by intention focus concentration, enabling access to more rarefied levels of the mind for communication with the spiritual realms for prophecy and guidance and to influence events. That is how knowledge of the healing powers of plants was first gained, how understanding was developed about the importance of honoring the four directions and the four basic elements: earth, air, fire, and water. Anyone who has ever been swept away by the beauty of a sunset or found an answer to a problem while communing with nature has caught a glimpse of the worlds that are open to indigenous peoples who foster this kind of knowing.

Spirituality's highest purpose is to touch a mystery beyond words, which is perceived only in silence and solitude, the Grandmothers say. Listening within the silence puts one in touch with the energy, vibration, and spiritual forces that are at the heart of Creation. The realms are real, not of the imagination, and can only be reached by a quiet mind and by practice. This does not mean there is a lack of critical thinking, only that thinking about the experience while in the moment stops the experience. The Grandmothers believe we must return to our inner spirit and the spirit of all things, which we have abandoned while looking elsewhere for happiness.

The Grandmothers know there has been an undeniable corruption of humanity's spirit. The global human family, a macrocosm of the tribal system, is lost in confusion and sickness. We are disconnected from ourselves and from the planet that nurtures us, body and soul. Violence and war have bred hunger, poverty, loss of culture, and a lack of understanding concerning basic human rights. Our waters, the blood of our Mother Earth, are often too polluted to drink, the air in some places too polluted to breathe. Do we really want it this way for ourselves, for future generations, they ask? We have lost the most fundamental teaching: that all life is sacred, all life is One. The Grandmothers say we must wake up from our trance before the Earth begins shaking.

Prophecies of each of the Grandmothers' traditions state that we are entering the Purification Times. The purification process is a natural cleansing of all the accumulated negativity caused by being materially instead of spiritually oriented. All of life must be honored and protected again, allowed its natural source of shelter and nourishment. Since all of life is connected, the Grandmothers believe that healing, quality of life, and spiritual evolvement are never separate from politics and consciousness. Culture that does not derive or base itself on nature's laws has no roots and can't survive long. Without a deep connection to nature, people drift, grow negative, and destroy themselves spiritually and physically. Deeply connected to nature, we see beauty everywhere, including within ourselves.

Each part of the world holds wisdom, a key to reigniting humanity's pure spark. The thirteen Grandmothers came in council to share their prayers, rituals, and ceremonies to create global healing and forge an alliance creating one voice. They speak of ways of bringing about sustainability, sovereignty, and a unified alliance among all the Earth's people in the interest of life and peace.

The Birth of the Grandmothers Council

The extraordinary women of the Grandmothers Council were first drawn together by an American woman named Jeneane Prevatt (who goes by the name Jyoti). Her doctoral studies had taken her to the C. G. Jung Institute in Zurich, where she became interested in the contributions indigenous traditions could make in "helping people to discover their innate wisdom and power." Jyoti is now the director of the Center for Sacred Studies, a nonprofit dedicated to sustaining indigenous ways of life through crosscultural education, spiritual practice, and exchange. (She also founded Kayumari, a spiritual community in the Sierra Nevada mountain range of California.)

Inspired by indigenous spirituality, Jyoti says that she began a sustained prayer to find a way to "preserve and apply the teachings of the original people." In response to her prayers, she experienced a series of visions, including one in which she saw a circle of Grandmothers coming together from different parts of the world. Jyoti felt she was being called to give these women a voice. Following the guidance of her visions, she turned to contacts she and members of her community had already established through years of visiting and learning from indigenous peoples around the globe, and Jyoti sent out letters of inquiry to sixteen women elders. In the letter she described her vision and asked each woman for her presence on the council. If one elder declined, she referred Jyoti to another.

All the Grandmothers who accepted said they knew deep within that they were meant to participate, even if at first they might have felt unworthy. They knew the Grandmothers from the Spirit World, the wise ones humanity has forgotten, were calling them to action. (For a more detailed account of how the Grandmothers Council came together, see the appendix.)

Jyoti had no idea how many Grandmothers should be on the council, and no one knew there was a specific number in the prophecy until they came together in council for the first time. Prophecy is traditionally revealed and confirmed over time, in bits and pieces and through many different people, with each revelation deepening its meaning. This was true for the Grandmothers themselves, as visions and prophecies continued to reveal their destined work together.

The Grandmothers first learned that thirteen was the correct number of council members when tears welled up in Yupik Grandmother Rita Pitka Blumenstein's eyes as she introduced herself on the first day of the gathering. She handed out thirteen stones and thirteen eagle feathers to each of the Grandmothers, a gift she had been holding and waiting to give for a very long time. The thirteen stones and thirteen eagle feathers had been given to Rita when she was nine years old by her great-grandmother, who told her to give them to the women of the Council of Grandmothers when they all finally met, a council Rita would someday be a part of.

The number thirteen is also considered a sacred number in each of the Grandmothers' traditions. During ancient times, the year was divided into thirteen months because there were thirteen full moons in a year, and a woman's cycle is intimately linked with the cycles of the moon. In those times, women were greatly honored because their bodies were synchronized with the heavens and able to create life, the same as Mother Earth.

The collective force of the thirteen Grandmothers, the result of their shared compassion and dedication to life, to all of nature and to the intelligence inherent in Creation, became apparent right away when large and small donations began pouring in, even before much was known about the direction the council would take. People worked without pay to make the gathering happen. Miraculously, $250,000 was raised in two years, from the time when Jyoti committed herself to bringing the council to life until they all met in New York for the first time. (This was the money needed to bring the Grandmothers and a select group of Western women elders together from the four corners of the Earth for a week, house them and offer each an honorarium, plus house three hundred conference participants.) Money came from grants, private donations, and fees from others who came to participate in the conference. Funding also came together for a documentary film chronicling the council's work. The idea for the council was being infused with a great deal of generosity, love, and faith.

Ancient Wisdom, Future Vision

By applying their ancient, indigenous ways of seeing and being to all the major issues of today, the Grandmothers hope to change the direction of the world and ensure eventual peace and prosperity for all the following generations. These spiritual leaders—shamans, medicine women, and channelers of sacred energy—address the essential elements in creating a healthy future: how to heal families, how to end war, the proper relationship between men and women, integrating traditional and indigenous medicine, maintaining the Earth's balance, and bringing forth the collective power of wise women by deepening our relationship with the feminine.

Through sharing their visions, prophecies, and ancient healing and nurturing ways, the Grandmothers hope to inspire others to more con-

sciously partake in the unfolding of Creation. As carriers of their tribes'
traditions, all these women elders are powerful; they are fierce in the
best sense. Their deep knowledge and reverence make them poets of life
and great storytellers. Even sitting within the potency of their silence,
much is transmitted. Their myths and stories, their ways of explaining
archetypes reveal multiple windows into the heart and psyche.

Another ancient Hopi prophecy, shared by many tribes, tells of the
beginning of the world, when the Creator created four races of four colors, each assigned a task that together would ensure a world where all
life was held in one sacred circle. The native peoples, the red people,
were entrusted with the guardianship of the Earth, the teachings of the
plants, foods, and healing herbs. The yellow race carried the knowledge
of air, of spiritual advancement through knowledge of the sky, wind,
and breath. The black people were given knowledge of the water, the
most adaptive and yet most powerful of the elements, the knowledge of
the depths of human emotion. The white people were given the knowl
edge of fire, which creates, consumes, and moves.

Breath, blood, and bones—at the most basic level not much distin-
guishes us one from the other. We all meet in the same place, the Grandmothers remind us. The Hopi prophecy states that not until all four
races of humanity come together will there be true peace. Until now, the
red race, the native peoples with their Earth-based wisdom, have been
excluded from the world's discourse. The Grandmothers helped to fulfill the Hopi prophecy, as all four races with their unique teachings
came together for the first time in all of history to find a way to create a
better world. They met with Western women elders from all walks of
life, hoping to reconnect with the principles that allowed the planet to
flourish for many thousands of years. They all came to the land of the
Iroquois, a land of pristine rivers and ancient mountains, from many
different countries but with one heart.

The sacred fire was to burn for seven days. As the Grandmothers approached the fire with their offerings, some were silent as they prayed,
some sang, some walked slowly around the fire circle, pausing at the
four directions. When Agnes Baker Pilgrim, the oldest living member of
her tribe, the Takelma Indians, a band along the Rogue River in southern

Oregon (and as the oldest Grandmother, the chosen spokesperson), circled the fire, the wind suddenly came up and swirled around the Grandmothers. Not one leaf on the surrounding trees even slightly stirred.

"The Grandmothers from the other side are here," Grandmother Agnes said, not at all surprised but deeply humbled. "They give their blessing."

PART ONE

The Grandmothers

Agnes Baker Pilgrim
Takelma Siletz
(GRANTS PASS, OREGON)

TEARS OF AWE AND GRATITUDE well up whenever Agnes Baker Pilgrim, world-renowned spiritual leader and Keeper of the Sacred Salmon Ceremony for her people, tells of the heartbreaking beauty and extraordinary nurturing power of the female salmon, as she sacrifices herself to fulfill her destiny. After the long and dangerous journey upstream to her place of origin, where she lays her eggs for the last time, the female salmon turns back downstream and begins to die. During her slow death, her flesh falls off into the water and nurtures other little fish. Then the remains of her body continue to nourish thirty-three kinds of birds and forty-four kinds of animals, who drink from the river and carry her minerals to replenish the land and surrounding vegetation.

At some point in the telling, the listener has become the salmon, so powerful are her words and images, drawn from thousands of years of ritual and ceremony to honor the Salmon People's sacred path. Worlds are opened to a level of unconditional giving rarely understood, and to the truth of our interdependence as only a tiny part of Creation.

"Legend tells us that the salmon were people shaped like us that lived in a beautiful city below the ocean floor," Grandmother Agnes says. "The spirit of the Salmon People chose to come back every spring and fall to feed the two-leggeds of this world. Lots of people say, 'Grandma Agnes, that's a terrible story!' But I tell them the Salmon People chose to sacrifice themselves to feed us."

Believing it was only fitting, Grandmother Agnes revived the Sacred Salmon Ceremony after it had been lost for over 150 years, after miners had arrived on the shores of southwestern Oregon and massacred the Indian people, nearly destroying in four years a culture that had survived for thousands. Mining debris began to pour down the rivers, greatly diminishing the salmon run and choking much of the freshwater fish that had been so abundant. As a result, the surrounding environment was thrown into shock. As they settled the land without any regard for nature, the miners and their families decimated the deer and elk populations and much of the area's natural resources. The rush for quick wealth unraveled nature's ways, which had long been supported through the respectful practices of the native tribes for tens of thousands of years.

"I am a voice for the voiceless . . . speaking for our Mother Earth."

The number of salmon returning upriver to spawn has increased dramatically since Grandmother Agnes's revival of the ceremony, and the people of the region are growing more connected with the land and opening essential connections within themselves as a result, she says. *National Geographic* magazine and Eastman Kodak have lent their support to the ceremony, as has Martha Stewart, who created greater awareness of the ceremony when she participated in it on her show.

Grandmother Agnes believes the ceremony opened a space for the healing energy of the Creator by offering prayers of gratitude to the Salmon People for giving up their lives to feed humanity. "I am trying to teach reciprocity," she says. "We two-leggeds are always taking and rarely giving back. Without reciprocity, the balance of nature is thrown off. Ritual and ceremony create the energy of reciprocity."

A spiritual elder of the Confederate Tribes of Siletz, Grandmother Agnes, who is honored as a living legend by the people of her region, has traveled the world, fighting for the planet and for endangered species.

"I am a voice for the voiceless," she says. "We are all speaking to an unseen world, speaking for our Mother Earth, trying to stop our spiritual blindness. We speak for the animal kingdom, for those in the waters, for the "four-leggeds" and the one-leggeds (the trees), the Bengal tiger, the camel, the elephant, the creepy crawlers. I pray our Creator hears us. The creatures have a right to be. The Creator gave us instructions about this and about how to be a long time ago. He told us the ways to take care of ourselves, what to eat and where to live. But now we are unbalanced.

We cut the green off our Mother's face. We pollute the water, Her blood. We do clearcut logging on the top of mountains, when the trees there are the ones that call the wind and the rain. Without the ancient trees at the top of our mountains, we are in trouble. The little trees can't do the same work as the old trees that have been destroyed."

Agnes Baker Pilgrim

Grandmother Agnes believes that with the brain, humanity was given a mandate from the Creator to be caretakers of all that came before and to keep the four elements—earth, air, water, and fire—in balance. "We have walked away from those teachings, and the planet is suffering," she says.

In 1982, Grandmother Agnes had cancer and was at death's door. She asked the Creator to let her live, because her family needed her and she believed she had a lot left to do in the world. She hasn't slowed down since. Her call to the spiritual path was initiated with a sense of restlessness that she felt even in dreamtime. She was forty-five. A force was pulling her toward a spiritual path, and she was told to cleanse her "inner self." She fought this inner calling because she didn't feel worthy to take the spiritual journey. What she came to experience during that time was a "dying to self." Still she fought the Creator all the way, until a friend advised her to stop resisting and surrender.

When she finally decided to follow the spiritual ways, she felt a large load fall off her shoulders. Her sight opened up and she could psychically see with her eyes closed. She vowed to walk the path in order to honor and respect her ancestors and the future generations, her parents and her children. She also vowed to fight for the well-being of her beloved Mother Earth and the sacred places of her people.

"The dominant society does not agree with the native peoples' idea of sacred; they desecrate our spiritual places. We must stop this spiritual blindness, this inability to see and feel the sacred around us," she says.

GRANDMOTHER AGNES was delivered into this world by her grandmother, a midwife. Her father was a chief. Her grandfather, Chief George Harney, was the first elected chief of the Confederated Tribes of Siletz. "As the daughter of the first elected chief," Grandmother Agnes explains, "my mother was considered a princess, though there is not a word for *princess* in my language. But she was respected in a very good way." The family was of the Siletz and Takelma Indians of the Table Rocks area, who lived along the Rogue River in southwestern Oregon for over twenty-two thousand years. The headwaters of the Siletz River were where her people were driven on the Trail of Tears. Takelma means in the native language "those dwelling along the river."

Grandmother Agnes's native name is Taowhywee, which means Morning Star. When she was visiting the Blood Reserve in Alberta, Canada, she was given another native name, Naibigwan, which means Dragonfly. In her tribe the dragonfly was known as the "Transformer." Legend tells of how, when the people of her tribe passed on, they returned as dragonflies.

"Dragonflies have been a phenomenal thing in my life," Grandmother Agnes says. "If you come to my house, you will see. I have them on my socks. They're in my hair, my curtains, on my towels, my aprons. I have them in all forms of candleholders and things hanging from the trees by my house. I think the ancestors are trying to tell me something!"

Grandmother Agnes grew up without electricity. The family of nine children was poor, as it was the Depression, but she never felt deprived or that she was missing anything because that was all she knew. From a young age, she worked with the native plants and in the family garden. "At first, we were given four plants to take care of. When I was old enough to go to school, I was responsible for four rows," she says.

By the time Grandmother Agnes graduated from high school, both of her parents had died and her brothers were her caregivers. When she became an adult, Grandmother Agnes worked as an assistant for a doctor in Portland, then as a scrub nurse in a local hospital. She met her husband in Portland. They married when she was twenty and had three children. After her first husband died, she married again and had three more children, in all three sons and three daughters. A widow a second time, she then married a Yurok man. Both her first and youngest sons have crossed over. Now she has eighteen grandchildren and twenty-seven great-grandchildren. The fifth generation of her family, a great-great-great-granddaughter was recently born. Grandmother Agnes is proud that all follow the traditional ways and walk a good path.

"We must stop this spiritual blindness, this inability to see and feel the sacred around us."

After working for the Indian Health Services for many years, Grandmother Agnes returned to college at age fifty, majoring in psychology and Native American studies. She also became an elder mentor at Southern Oregon University, where she is an alumna and helped to found Konanway Nika Tillicum (All My Relations) Youth Academy. The academy teaches native protocol, academics, and drama (to help young people overcome shyness). The students live on campus for nineteen days and, in addition to learning about native culture, are introduced to the college experience. Over the years, Grandmother Agnes has been honored for her leadership and community service and as an educator, keeper of traditional ways, and source of inspiration locally, statewide, nationally, and internationally.

The oldest of the thirteen Grandmothers, Grandmother Agnes was asked to chair their council. Addressing the council during its first meeting, she said, "The empowerment, knowledge, wisdom, caring, and sharing around the table is magnificent. I felt you all before I saw you. One of the beautiful things I can say is that the Creator is on our side because we are walking our talk. That is a power in itself."

Grandmother Agnes believes the Grandmothers are of the warrior essence that has been handed down from generation to generation. "The Ancient Ones are speaking through our voices," she says. "From the get-go, this council originated from the Spirit World. Every one of us has been called. Through our prayers, we can touch the hearts of the people. We can help stop spiritual blindness around the world. Our prayers can turn the terrorists around to a more positive way of life. We have been brought from the four corners of the world for this work. We can be the voice of strength, encouragement, and love, fighting for peace. Remember, even water dripping on a rock can make a difference."

Grandmother Agnes's greatest hope is to protect and preserve the beauty in the world we have today so that the seventh generation from now can enjoy it as well. She believes we are all being prompted by the seven generations behind us to ensure that end. As she is fond of saying, "Yesterday is history, tomorrow is a mystery, today is our gift, and we better use it wisely."

Bernadette Rebienot
Omyèné
(GABON, AFRICA)

BORN IN LIBREVILLE, GABON, of the Omyèné linguistic community, Bernadette Rebienot lost her mother when she was five years old and was raised by her father and her grandmother. She was very young and still had a child's innocence when her first vision came to her in the midst of a family gathering. She saw her father's friend die in the water. When she told her father, he asked her what she was talking about. His questioning tone caused her to fall silent. She didn't feel comfortable answering him.

Even when her visions came to pass, Bernadette kept quiet about the unbidden images she continued to see in her mind, an ability she had inherited. Her grandmother was a twin, and it was believed she was given many special gifts as a result. Bernadette's grandmother was infused with the traditional medicine ways, practiced by the Pygmies for thousands of years. Her specialties were difficult births and healing fractures. Through her grandmother, who taught her about all the plants that grew around their yard, some of which grew naturally and some her grandmother planted for medicinal purposes, Bernadette was introduced very early to the plant world. She was taught that the plants were a special gift from the ancestors and must be protected for future generations. Her grandmother was always telling Bernadette to "pay attention to tomorrow" and "respect the forest."

Because her mother had died, when Bernadette was of school age she was given to the local nuns to be raised at the convent. Her grandmother believed strongly that education was a passport and conferred a sense of dignity. At the convent, Bernadette began to share her visions with her friends as play. But then she became seriously ill. The right side of her face was affected. She lived in excruciating pain and was forced to stay in darkness, since being in light made her ill.

The illness lasted three years, despite the efforts of modern medicine, and the family grew increasingly worried. With her grandmother's insistence, they decided to try the traditional medicine approach. In a psychic vision, the Pygmy master, whom they had sought out for healing, saw that Bernadette had a special gift and that she had to accept the illness as her path to initiation as a medicine woman. Initiation in her culture means a spiritual awakening and pertains mostly to healing the spirit, rather than the physical body.

"There are two kinds of people, the initiated and those who are not initiated, people who have spiritual knowledge and those who don't," Grandmother Bernadette says. "The path of illumination for the initiated allows another vision of life, another way of understanding the realities of life and one's own life. Mankind is universally the same. Spirituality, which inhabits us all, is equally universal. It is just up to each person whether or not to choose that path."

Traditional medicine in Grandmother Bernadette's culture accepts that humans actually have two bodies: a physical body and a spiritual body. Practitioners of traditional medicine accept this natural process, which looks at people in their relationship with nature and the cosmos. When there is disease, it is the person who is ill that is treated, not the illness itself.

"Spirituality, which inhabits us all, is equally universal. It is just up to each person whether or not to choose that path."

"Disease is a foreign thing. It inhabits us to bother us into making necessary spiritual changes," Grandmother Bernadette explains. "So the spiritual body is always treated along with the physical body; whereas the scientific world only recognizes physical disease and any healing measures end there. The spiritual side of a person is not their concern. In Africa, the two sides are considered complementary and are not enemies. After all, both are about healing the human being."

At least 80 percent of the population of Africa go to traditional healers. Grandmother Bernadette believes that throughout the world both the traditional and scientific communities must respect and accept each other and, if that condition is fulfilled, we are working toward the healing of humanity.

Originally, her great love of life and her love of dancing proved to be an obstacle to Grandmother Bernadette's initiation, for she did not want to assume the responsibilities of a medicine woman. But, in the end, the illness gave her no choice. Since she had to avoid light, she could not continue her life as usual. Finally, she had to accept her initiation. The first Pygmy master, who was considered a great man, asked three others, four masters in all, to participate in her initiation rite, which was a supreme honor.

In most indigenous cultures there is a special healing plant that is essential to their medicine ways and used in initiation ceremonies. The traditional healing plant for Gabon is called Iboga, which was used in Grandmother Bernadette's initiation and is found in the Gabon forests.

Iboga has a long story that goes back thousands of years and originated with two groups of Pygmies, who lived in the stunningly lush paradise of Gabon's primeval rain forest that covers twenty-two million square kilometers (over eight million square miles) of land. To outsiders, the dense damp forest, with its water-laden trees constantly dripping and the haunting sounds of the many birds and animals, was often seen as an inhospitable, lonely, and frightening place. With no understanding that the lingering soulful cry of the chameleon was actually telling them there was honey in the trees, that everything in the forest was in communication and providing for all needs, outsiders who were beginning to colonize the region held no reverence for such a creation and no respect for its natives, the Pygmies. In contrast, the Pygmies have always been in constant praise of their magical paradise as their provider, protector, and deity. They have always lived in their forest world with a profound and joyful intimacy and shared a secret language with the forest that remains a mystery to any outsider.

Today the forest is in imminent danger from logging companies that are plundering this jewel of nature at a fast pace. The biggest trees of this pristine forest, which are hundreds of years old, are being cut down, permanently destroying the delicate ecological balance of the forest—all to supply a demand for parquet floors and furniture made of tropical wood. Poachers are using the logging roads to kill elephants, gorillas, and chimpanzees for the delicacy of their meat, and now there is the possibility that the meat is spreading AIDS and Ebola. The local population is endangered as their food supply dwindles, and most doubt that the forest animals can survive the poachers' encroachment.

As the delicate balance of the forest is disrupted, one of the most important medicines the forest produces, the plant used in Grandmother Bernadette's initiation, could be in danger of becoming scarce. Iboga, one of the many gifts of the forest, was discovered when the Pygmies observed its effects on certain animals that ate the plant's roots. They learned that Iboga allows a person to work for long hours without fatigue and to go a long time without feeling hunger. It is also an aphrodisiac, as well as a healer of the spiritual body.

"In Gabon, when the Grandmothers speak, the president listens. There is war all around us, but there is no war in Gabon."

"Iboga is a cultural treasure," Grandmother Bernadette explains. "We are the holders of the plant's secrets and don't accept its being called a hallucinogenic. Iboga is therapeutic spiritually, a plant about meditation. It allows us to relieve ourselves of past emotional memories, resolve inner conflict, to know where the blocks are within ourselves, and then to reconcile with oneself."

Traditional medicine practitioners feel that the scientific community does not understand Iboga the way it should be understood. After centuries of observation they have found that the plant can heal alcoholism, that it fights addiction to certain drugs, and that it can be taken without creating any dependency.

"Iboga does not lead you to want to take it," Grandmother Bernadette explains. "In fact, it takes courage to take it, because it makes you look at yourself so deeply and honestly. It will be a part of tomorrow's medicine."

During her first initiation with Iboga as a teenager, Grandmother Bernadette was able to see everything that was going to happen to her in the future, and her health returned. Under the supervision of her master teacher, she slowly began to use her gifts, finally understanding and accepting her own destiny and her own spirituality, which led her to becoming a healer. These skills, which she developed under her master's tutelage, she has applied as a teacher, therapist, and master of the Iboga Bwiti Rite and of Women's Initiations. The people call her by her spirit name, which means "awaited one, expected for a long time."

"What I do today does not surprise me," Grandmother Bernadette explains. "I saw it all a long time ago. I didn't deduct anything from all I saw, and I haven't added anything. The temple that we build is from all that is inside us. This little voice within that each one of us has is our own adviser."

Grandmother Bernadette soon became well known in her country. She has been president of the Health Department of Traditional Medicine since 1994 and has participated in many conferences in that capacity at the international level. She is now widowed, the mother of ten living children and twenty-three grandchildren.

For centuries, the women of Gabon have regularly gathered in the forest to share their visions, to pray for world peace and for the well-being of their people. "In Gabon," Grandmother Bernadette says, "when the Grandmothers speak, the president listens. There is war all around us, but there is no war in Gabon."

Addressing the Council of Grandmothers for the first time, Grandmother Bernadette said it felt like a dream to be sitting around the table with these women. She had seen them all while in a trance, thirteen Grandmothers from around the world speaking with one voice.

"The spirits of the forest of Gabon have said that we can't go backwards anymore. We can't have fear anymore. Time is short. Time is calling us. Spirit exists. It is much stronger than the body. In the words of the Grandmothers from Africa, spirituality is no different among the races. No one chooses where they are born. Only destiny. We accept that. We all share ancestors, because humanity is humanity. Think of our sisters who fought and are dead from fighting for the human race. Let us stand for all who have fought for peace.

"This morning, as I watched a deer in these beautiful woods, a spirit called my name twice," she said. "The voice of the spirit assured me this is very, very big work we Grandmothers are doing."

Flordemayo

Mayan

(NICARAGUA/NEW MEXICO)

FLORDEMAYO, a Mayan elder and *Curandera Espiritu* (spiritual healer), was born on the Nicaragua/Honduras border in the highlands of Central America, where her mother, who was widowed when Flordemayo was two-and-a-half, was a midwife and healer. The youngest of fifteen children, all of whom were gifted in some way, Flordemayo was the only child in her family with the gift of seeing visions. In the Mayan culture, to be born with the ability to heal and to receive visions is greatly honored. It is why some Central Americans have many children; parents keep hoping for a child born with the gift.

"Before she died," Grandmother Flordemayo recalls, "my mother told me that I was born to 'close her eyes.' In other words, my mother could rest in peace knowing the healing work was to continue."

Nearly every morning at breakfast, Flordemayo's mother would ask all the children about their dreams and was able to track where each child was by the sorts of dreams they were having. Since she began talking at a very early age, Flordemayo was able to participate in the discussions and let her mother know of her visions at a very young age.

At four years of age, Flordemayo became her mother's apprentice. Her initiation happened one midnight, during a full moon, when her mother said, "Daughter, wake up. The stork is coming!"

Together, they ran in the moonlight to the neighbors to attend to a birth. Flordemayo was being put to work, and from then on always went with her mother to all the births. Her job was to wait, most times in the kitchen by a wood fire, where she'd be offered a treat of hot cocoa or milk from the clay stoves, until the baby was born. Then her mother would bring the baby to her, all rolled up in a blanket like a sausage, and ask her to read the baby's life history. Spiritual beings told her what to say. This was something she loved doing.

Growing up, Flordemayo learned the healing art of the curandera in the traditional way, passed down orally from mother to daughter, generation after generation.

"That's how I work, with the spirit of my mother and my grandmother right beside me," Grandmother Flordemayo explains.

The lineage of the *curanderismo* is five hundred years old and began with the arrival of the Europeans and slaves from Africa, when it evolved into a mixture of African, Christian, and indigenous teachings. Midwives, bone setters, masseuses, and herbalists can all be curanderas. Curanderisma is practiced in Mexico and throughout Central and South America. Traditional medicine is strictly indigenous, but *curanderismo* is a mix of African, Christian, and indigenous.

In 1960, when in her early teens, Grandmother Flordemayo moved with her mother and several of her siblings to New York City. The political climate in her country was getting dangerous. Moving to New York was a shock for Flordemayo. She didn't know the language and could not read or write in her own. Her mother had kept her from formal schooling in order not to interfere with her learning the healing ways. For many years after moving to New York, Flordemayo was not involved with the teachings.

A new consciousness is to be created that will combine the accomplishments of the mind and the deep wisdom of the heart, which is the key to a prosperous and sustainable future for all.

But when her mother became seriously ill, she again taught her daughter the healing ways, and Flordemayo began to develop the ability to see disease. Just before she was to marry a man she met in New York City, her mother passed over. For years after her mother's death, Flordemayo felt very alone, stranded in a culture she didn't understand and that didn't understand her. Yet during that time she had many revelations and felt the presence of her mother always with her. She was being divinely guided and became adept at helping others release negative energy.

In 1974, when she was in her early twenties, a bus full of indigenous elders traveled across the United States to the Adirondacks, spreading the teachings that we are all One, that there is no real separation, and that we must begin to take care of our planet. The bright yellow bus, with colorful flags flying from the windows and named Four Arrows, stopped right in front of Flordemayo's house in the Adirondacks, where she had moved with her husband. Flordemayo was stunned when someone asked her who she was and where was her tribe. She was confused by the elders' questions but offered to get on the bus and show them the way to the community college. She quickly became their translator and part of the happening.

The elders were also gathering to bring healing energy to North America, in order to initiate the fulfillment of the ancient prophecy of the Eagle and the Condor, which promised that one day gatherings of elders would be formed to share their different traditions, medicines, and healing ways in order to pass on this ancient knowledge and wisdom to all of humanity. Prophecy stated that it would be the People of the Center (Central America) who would facilitate the movement of energy from the south (the People of the Condor) to the north (the People of the Eagle), in order to bring the two groups, north and south, together again.

The prophecy states that "Those from the center make us unite the Eagle of the north and the Condor of the south. We will meet with our relatives, because we are one as are the fingers of our hand."

In the times before countries and international borders, the peoples of the Americas would come together to share wisdom, knowledge, and experience. Separated by distance, time, and the lack of rapid transportation, these sharings could only happen once every century or so. The ancient elders knew that, at some point in the future, this free flow of culture would be interrupted, and that the peoples would develop independently in the direction of their greater tendencies and forget or diminish the influence of their brothers and sisters of other regions.

The peoples of North America, represented by the Eagle, developed in the direction of ceremony and spiritual knowledge. The peoples of Central America developed the knowledge of timekeeping and astronomy, creating an accurate system of calendars and an advanced understanding of the movement of planets and stars. The peoples of South America, represented by the Condor, developed agricultural methods and knowledge of medicinal plants and are responsible for most of the popular vegetable foods of the world today.

For the greater good of the Americas and their peoples, it would become imperative that the peoples come together again, so no group would be left behind. The time the ancient elders had spoken of in their prophecy is upon us now.

Grandmother Flordemayo is dedicated to this very time in history, which prophecy states is when the Eagle and the Condor will at last begin to fly together again, wing tip to wing tip, and the peoples will come together to share their knowledge and to save one another. A new consciousness is to be created, as a result, that will combine the accomplishments of the mind and the deep wisdom of the heart, the key to a prosperous and sustainable future for all. But first the two peoples must learn to understand each other.

"Prophecy also states that it will be the women who walk with the power," says Grandmother Flordemayo. "We have an incredible journey and responsibility as women. All of our life, we are caretakers, walking with the Mother. We carry this within our being. For women to have the freedom in the heart to be able to express ourselves spiritually is very, very important. We must learn to stay balanced in the moment and give each moment 100 percent of our prayer. When we go off balance and get rocked by life, we need to bring ourselves back quickly to the moment, one moment at a time. We can't do that by hoping for things to change tomorrow. We must give each moment 100 percent of our care right in the moment. This can be very difficult at times, but the spirit of the feminine is here now in a very powerful way."

Grandmother Flordemayo teaches that the way to balance is to feel the love and nourishing energy at the heart of the Earth move through the soles of our feet, then invoke the heart of the heavens to move in through the crown of our heads and allow the two energies to meet in the center of our being. Finally, we must allow the energy thus created to move out as far as it needs to go.

Grandmother Flordemayo has traveled the world as a bridge of light to pray in this way and sees that people around the world are calling for prayer, because there is an incredible need for prayer. Our different languages and religions are not an obstacle and have nothing to do with true prayer, which is honoring and humbling, she says.

"We live now with chaos and intensity. There is just so much out there to see and to witness and to hear. Centering within and prayer are two ways to control fear," Grandmother Flordemayo says. "Pray with every breath."

Flordemayo is the name of a healing plant, and the name means "Flower of the Dawn." The flower petals can be pastel pink, white, yellow, or purple. The fragrant flower is delicate, lasting only for one day. In traditional medicine it is a woman's plant and is used for lactation and for restoring the womb after birth. It is also believed to retard AIDS.

In the desert of New Mexico, the Institute of Natural and Traditional Medicine grows thousands of medicinal herbs from which is produced a line of traditional healing products. The institute owns an organic seed bank, collected from all over the world, that ensures growth for the future if needed. Flordemayo believes it is time for there to be no secrets about the plants and their medicinal properties, no more barriers to others' understanding of their uses, and that it is also time to introduce the children of the world to the medicine. This would be the first time in history that traditional healers would be putting their secret knowledge out into the world. They are now of the mind that they want people to take this knowledge and move to make changes with it quickly.

"We have the power to regenerate with the plants," Grandmother Flordemayo says. "But we must honor, respect, preserve, and pray for them. We have a relationship with the spirit of the plant, the spirit of the sacred waters. We must take care of these things for the generations to come. Ritual, ceremony, and astronomy teach when it is best to plant the seeds. We have a strong body of teachers behind us for this work. The peoples of Central America already know how to make emergency first-aid medicine. If we could start all over again and be empowered, we could give solutions to modern-day ailments.

"It has taken only one hundred years to almost totally lose this wisdom," Grandmother Flordemayo says. "We can't waste any more time on this anymore. We all have incredible responsibilities."

Grandmother Flordemayo began studying with the elders she met on the yellow bus and feels her Mayan heritage is the keystone of her work. Now recognized by the Mayans as a priestess, she also works with sacred breath, the sacred herbal baths, Mayan "invisible surgery," the laying on of hands, and remote healing. She rebalances the physical, emotional, and spiritual bodies and the subtle energy systems known as the aura and chakras.

Grandmother Flordemayo is also a Sun Dancer, a commitment she says she made to the Spirit to dance for the benefit of nations. The medicine of the Sun Dance is so sacred that it can't be elaborated upon.

"Basically my teaching is to be human, honor people, and be free in the heart."

Grandmother Flordemayo also conducts the traditional Mayan healing ceremonies, practicing the "Path of the Thirteen Sacred Centers." She gives workshops and classes and speaks at conferences worldwide. She has put together a program to introduce the teachings of the curanderismo to people from all walks of life.

"Spirit guides me in all my work," Grandmother Flordemayo says. "Basically my teaching is to be human, honor people, and be free in the heart."

She is director of the Institute of Natural and Traditional Medicine, a school and healing center. She is president of the Confederation of Indigenous Peoples of the Americas, a nonprofit organization dedicated to uniting native peoples everywhere and to bringing their message to all humanity. She has been the recipient of the prestigious Martin de la Cruz award for her healing work in the world. She and her husband have two children and now have three grandchildren.

As the Grandmothers met in council in the land of the Eagle, Grandmother Flordemayo offered a prayer as a way of introducing herself.

"In the name of the heart of the heavens, heart of wind, heart of fire, thank you beloved spirit of fire, nurturer of generations, Spirit that makes us who we are. I honor you. Thank you for the light that guides us, for showing us who we are—the light that burns within us, that has *Flordemayo* brought us together.

"Thank you circle, spirit of beauty, fire, Mother/Father Creator of humanity. Thank you for taking us from the beginning of time. Here we stand before you. My heart feels the beauty, the burning. We are humans with this fire, and we are nobody without this fire.

"Thank you spirit of Grandmothers that guides us, that will not allow us to fail. Thank you for guidance. I honor you. Thank you for allowing me to be in this sacred circle at this sacred time. It is so vital to put the word out about our coming together spiritually. In fact, it is imperative. We are at the eleventh hour."

Margaret Behan

Arapaho/Cheyenne

(MONTANA)

MARGARET BEHAN, Red Spider Woman, was born on the fourth of July into the Beaver Clan, on her mother's side, part of the Cheyenne Nation of Oklahoma. Her father's side of the family was half Cheyenne, half Arapaho, and part of the Rabbit Lodge.

"Even before I was born, I was prayed for," Grandmother Margaret says. "My mother wanted to have another baby, so my grandfather had a peyote ceremony. I was the third generation to be conceived through the medicine, and I have been brought up with the medicine. Peyote has been an integral part of my life."

Grandmother Margaret was always taught that peyote is a sacrament and must never be used just to get high. "It is a healing medicine," she says. "No one can get addicted. Since it is very bitter tasting, few would want to do it for fun. It is a choice to eat the medicine peyote and use it in ceremony and with protocol.

"When I was little, my grandfather put up a tipi for me and held a ceremony for my life," Grandmother Margaret says. "In Cheyenne, such a thing is expressed as, 'He planted prayers for me.' My grandfather could see into the future that peyote would be of great benefit to people."

Grandmother Margaret is always touched by the stories of people who have been healed by peyote, stories she grew up with. Once, when her mother fell off a horse and broke her hip, the doctors wanted to break the bone again to have it mend correctly. But Grandmother Margaret's grandfather wouldn't let them. Instead, he held a prayer ceremony, and her mother walked again.

When he was eight, her son had a high heart rate. The doctors said that he needed to be sent all the way to Boston's Children's Hospital, and Grandmother Margaret didn't have the money it would take to travel there.

"My grandfather and uncles did the ceremony, and the doctors couldn't believe that my son was completely well afterwards," Grandmother Margaret recalls. "The heart specialist was excited and came to see us because he had never seen such a thing. When the doctors had given up on my sister-in-law, who had Crohn's disease, we called a meeting. Crohn's is physical, but in our view it is the emotions that cause it. By the time the ceremony was over, she had rid herself of a lot of the poison. Before our eyes, she was healed. Again, the doctors couldn't believe it. Crohn's is supposed to be incurable. All my life I knew these miracles."

Peyote is a medicine that creates a sense of well-being and facilitates rich and colorful visions that illuminate the unconscious and reveal the source of the physical problem. The plant, part of the cactus family, is considered sacred, a divine "messenger," because it enables an individual to communicate directly with God, without the mediation of a priest. As a spiritual medicine, it puts an individual in touch with the God within and back into balance with the Earth. For many, it is seen as a teacher and a way of life. It is said that, if peyote is used correctly, all other medicines are superfluous. When healing occurs on the spiritual levels of being, the healing is permanent.

Native Americans were introduced to peyote by the indigenous peoples of Mexico. Peyote became the subject of controversy, suppression, and persecution with the arrival of the new settlers, even though taking peyote without ceremony as a way of "getting high" was and still is considered a sacrilege among the Native American tribes that revere it. As more and more settlers arrived, the visions created by peyote were enabling the tribes to maintain connection and community, as their territories and ways of life were being taken over.

Grandmother Margaret's grandfather helped legalize peyote in 1918. A white couple, desperate for help for their dying baby, came to her grandfather for a cure. Her people had never doctored a white person, but her grandfather and uncles agreed to do a medicine ceremony and the baby lived. Afterward, the child was raised by his parents to "Never forget the Indians. They did their magic for you. Never forget them!" The baby grew up to become a lawyer and then a senator. In 1918, he met with Margaret's grandfather and told him he wanted to legalize the medicine ceremony, but in order to do so he had to put it under the auspices of the Native American Church, which he helped to establish in order to protect their medicine ways. With the passage of a 1994 amendment to the American Indian Religious Freedom Act of 1978, use of peyote in certain native ceremonies became legal from as far north as North Dakota on down through Mexico. Before 1978, all Native American ceremonies were illegal, whether they involved peyote or not. (For decades, the First Amendment did not cover Native American religious freedom.)

Margaret
Behan

GRANDMOTHER MARGARET'S PARENTS were migrant workers and had to leave their eight children to be raised by their parents, Margaret's grandparents. Margaret was the youngest. Her grandparents were in the Wild West Show in the 1920s, when her mother was a little girl. Grandmother Margaret and her siblings were raised in mission and government boarding schools.

"My parents were not able to be there for me," Grandmother Margaret recalls. "But, in our culture, we don't have aunts and uncles. We have a lot of mothers and fathers, so I have been parented, even though my own often needed to be absent."

Margaret's mother taught her beadwork and how to make buckskin dresses for her dolls. She also taught her about the sacred designs of her tribe and what they meant. Making dolls became Grandmother Margaret's artistic expression and, as an adult, she has earned many honors with her sculptures.

When Grandmother Margaret was five, she was sent to boarding school. "My parents would come to visit me and sing songs and tell the stories to me, so that I wouldn't forget my culture and my heritage," she recalls. "My father would tell me how the Creator loved us so much that he gave us a star and the star was the fire, so we are the Star People. He also told me that the Eagle is really an angel, and I should always pray to him. Those gifts from the Creator have helped me to be here now."

Grandmother Margaret's life was not an easy one. She began drinking at an early age. In the beginning, she had to force herself to take a drink, because she wanted desperately to feel like she fit in with her friends. She became a battered wife and had a difficult time raising her three children. She didn't know where to go for help or what to do. It was hard for her to ask for help for herself, though she was always giving to others. Finally she asked her uncle to create a ceremony for her.

Peyote is a sacred medicine that facilitates rich and colorful visions that illuminate the unconscious and reveal the source of a physical problem.

"During the ceremony, the roadman, who is the leader of the ceremony, has his own fireplace altar. Each person in the ceremony can look into the roadman's fire and receive their own vision," Grandmother Margaret explains. "In my vision, I saw a crescent moon that was all shattered, cracked all over. Immediately, I thought something even worse was going to happen in my life, and I got scared. As he was leading the ceremony, my uncle was watching me the whole time. He saw that I was scared. But I kept going, kept praying. By that point, I couldn't give up."

Then Grandmother Margaret saw that her altar was cracked and badly damaged. Everyone else saw it, too, and became happy. They told her it was evidence that the spirit helpers were there, that they had come to help her.

"From then on, I really understood that I could ask for help for myself," she says. "I could feel the presence of Spirit. I felt so comfortable, so taken care of. Just remembering that feeling helps me now."

As Grandmother Margaret continued to stare into the fire altar, she had a vision of herself in a ragged dress, but with brand new moccasins and leggings on. One foot was in dirt and the other on grass. While she looked down at her shoes, her uncle blew his eagle-bone whistle. Again, everyone was happy, and Grandmother Margaret thought she must be crazy. What were they all happy about? Her uncle had seen the same vision and said the ragged dress actually meant the opposite. The dress was new and her shoes were old.

"It's easier to explain in our language," Margaret says. "In visions, everything appears opposite. I began then to learn about seeing signs in ceremony."

When her mother was dying, she asked Grandmother Margaret to prepare four ceremonies before she left this world. Her sisters have helped. All the relatives came and brought the medicine. Inside the tipi, everyone was happy.

"It was all so wonderful," Grandmother Margaret remembers. "I was amazed, and then I knew that Spirit was very powerful to do these things in my life."

After her mother's death, Grandmother Margaret's life fell apart, and she asked herself over and over why her life had to be like that when she believed so deeply that the ceremonies would protect her. "I thought by now that the ceremonies were forever taking care of me. But I'd become an alcoholic."

One New Year's Day, Grandmother Margaret went into a ceremony to ask to become sober. She had always been told never to play with her prayers, that she had to mean it when she asked for help. She wanted to try to see if her prayer was real, if she was playing with it or if a cure could happen.

Soon after the ceremony, Grandmother Margaret began meeting sober people and knew that the medicine was true and working in her life. Then Margaret and her husband entered a treatment center together. After two weeks, he left, but Margaret stayed. She was determined to become sober.

While in treatment, her counselor asked her three questions that became burned in her mind. "She first asked me to look at how I saw myself in my environment, then how I looked at myself in the mirror, and finally she asked me to look at how I treated myself," Grandmother Margaret explains.

Though she wanted to magically become sober in an instant, she learned it was going to be a long and painful, not magical process. As she learned to face herself, Grandmother Margaret discovered that her hatred against herself served to oppress her. She needed to transform her poor self-esteem. And she realized she had to leave her husband in order to stay sober.

"I was really having to face myself," Grandmother Margaret says. "And face my understanding of Spirit, the ceremonies, and what I had asked for. That's when I really understood and believed at a deeper level."

During the time at the treatment center, Grandmother Margaret was offered a scholarship to be a substance abuse counselor by the director of the program, but she turned it down. She was an artist and resisted seeing herself as a counselor.

Two weeks after leaving treatment, Grandmother Margaret received a devastating phone call. Her son-in-law, who was an alcoholic, had taken his life, despite being in treatment to become sober. Two of her grandsons suddenly didn't have a father.

Needing support for herself, Grandmother Margaret asked for a meeting. "During the ceremony, I saw in the fire that I had to go back and learn about the enemy. My grandfather had always told me to learn about the enemy. Know what they eat. Know what they smell like, what they do. So I went back to the director crying and asked for the scholarship she had offered, so that I could learn about chemical dependency. I honored what I saw in the fire and my prayers."

Though she had to live in poverty in order to go to school and did without a lot of things, Grandmother Margaret was determined to finish her schooling. She had faith that Spirit had shown her the path she should take.

When Grandmother Margaret at last took charge of her life, everything opened up for her. By the time she had to choose her internship, she had been sober for three years. As a Native American woman, she had many opportunities. Ultimately, she wanted to help her own people and counsel in her own language. She also cleared up all the loose ends in her life by finalizing her divorce and solidifying her relationship with her children. By then, she had an empty nest. Finally, Grandmother Margaret decided to move to Montana.

After moving to Montana, where she knew only her niece, Grandmother Margaret spent time being completely alone. Again she was challenged when she discovered the job she had anticipated was not there for her when she arrived. Someone else had taken her position. So she created a taco stand, and people came to help her, seeming to be drawn by her presence. At first she couldn't see what was really going on, and then spiritual people, who usually stayed hidden and never talked to ordinary people, began to come to her and introduce her to their worlds.

Margaret Behan

"I knew I was having an introduction," she says. "I had three years of struggle, yet on the other hand I was meeting this beautiful other world of my Cheyenne people."

During this time, Grandmother Margaret became involved with psychodrama and discovered it had many similarities to the ceremonies and medicine ways, which also dealt first with the emotional and spiritual component of a disease.

"Psychodrama has immediate results," Grandmother Margaret explains. "If someone is dealing with anger, they go through the whole process of being angry. The counselor follows them all the way through. Medicine men and women do the same thing."

Psychodrama became an important tool in her healing work with trauma and substance abuse. Within a year, Grandmother Margaret was being invited around the country to be a presenter. She now gives workshops and retreats for all ages. She takes a unique approach to alcoholism by teaching about the early stages. Usually patients aren't seen until the later stages. Her approach is to talk about the difference between experimenting with alcohol and forcing oneself to drink because of a need to fit in with the crowd. Wanting to belong but feeling insecure is the first stage and a warning sign of alcoholism, she says. Drugs are taken for the same reason. She found that women weren't conscious of what they were doing to themselves by forcing themselves to drink.

As a fifth-generation survivor of the Sand Creek Massacre of 1864, considered by many to be the most egregious massacre in American history, Grandmother Margaret is researching generational trauma and the trauma of loss and grief, danger and fear, and hatred and chaos. Besides her acclaimed artistry of creating dolls, Grandmother Margaret is an author, poet, and playwright. She is a Cheyenne traditional dancer and a dance leader in powwows.

Margaret became a grandmother seventeen years ago and received the Grandmother blessing, which is her tribe's ordination into grandmotherhood. She introduced herself to the Grandmothers Council by singing the Turtle Song, a song taught to her by her grandmother. Then she told the Grandmothers that she got to the council because of the way she changed her life around. Now she feels she has a lot of people to sit in council and be brave for.

Grandmother Margaret's vision for the Grandmothers Council is seeing freedom for all from deprivation. She wants to free her people from alcohol and drug abuse and addiction.

"It has only been the last two hundred years that we have become chemically dependent. We can turn back to being the very powerful people we were. Powerful people are free and liberated people. We need to be liberated from addiction and liberated from society's judgments. Even walking in the mountains is a high. Picking the wild turnips is a sacred practice. We have to remember that again."

Addressing the Grandmothers, she said, "I know the ancient ways that we bring to this table from each of our traditions will make a difference."

Rita Pitka Blumenstein
Yupik
(ARCTIC CIRCLE)

YUPIK ELDER, Grandmother Rita Pitka Blumenstein, is the first person in Alaska to be certified as a traditional medicine doctor, and she never went to school. Instead, Rita grew up immersed in the powerful teachings of her grandmothers and great-grandmothers, the wise women elders of her people.

"I grew up with grandmothers, walked with grandmothers, and learned with grandmothers. I may not carry it as they did, but just a little bit. I feel connected to all the Grandmothers of the universe. My urge to share their teachings is strong," Grandmother Rita says. "I feel the world is ready to explode through the spirit of the Grandmothers and reach far out into the universe."

Grandmother Rita was born on a fishing boat. Her family was from the village of Tununak, located on the northeast coast of Nelson Island, a four-square-mile island in southwestern Alaska. The biting cold and barren tundra made for a hard life for the Yupiks. With no forests or trees, the Yupiks said special prayers for the return of the driftwood each year, and they relied on the animal spirits for help. As a result of their intense struggles for survival, they became a strong, close-knit and spiritual people. Yupik translates as "real people." When the Jesuits arrived on their shores, the Yupiks resisted all attempts at conversion. The shamans and the cultural traditions were too powerful.

After World War II, the U.S. government officially attempted to destroy the culture by eliminating gaming and fishing rights and establishing native schools where children were forbidden to speak their mother

tongue. The old ways of surviving on the tundra were deliberately and systematically wiped out.

Rita
Pitka
Blumenstein

Grandmother Rita's Yupik name means "Tail End Clearing of the Pathway to the Light." "I caught the tail end of the old ways," Grandmother Rita explains. "The ceremonies, the potlatch are old ways. There were ceremonies for the four seasons, mask ceremonies, prayers to the universe, ceremonies regarding the shamans' competition. That ceremony would scare me when I was little, because I didn't understand what it was about. I can see now, today, that all that happened back then was for this purpose, for this life we are living today. It was for my work now. The ceremonies were about what all our ancestors were doing for the future, for future use. We just didn't know back then that meant today."

Grandmother Rita believes we all come to the Earth from a seed, that every one of us, including generations to come, are planted on this Earth, into this world. We planned who our parents were going to be and what our life was going to be before we came here.

"My mother taught me that her tummy was my first world," Grandmother Rita says. "And whatever she did while I was in her was something I learned. Being in the mother's womb is like being under the ice, unsure of the light and hearing things but not clearly."

Yupiks believe learning begins while the body is developing inside the mother's womb. Whatever the mother does during the time of gestation has an impact on the child. So there are teachings about how to be with the baby before it is born. Yupiks believe it is significant that we are born very small and grow slowly, not eating right away, slowly developing our awareness of the world.

The design of Grandmother Rita's drum, which took her two years to make by hand, is meant to be like a womb. Each design, each symbol has significance. On it, the four directions are honored. The eye is the eye of the universe, the awareness of the universe. The sky is honored. Inside the circle is the symbol for hope. The drum is made of birch. The name of the birch tree in Yupik means "strong," because birch is used for everything: to make canoes, baskets, syrup, and sugar. From the inner bark, the Yupiks make their medicine for cancer; from the outer bark they make a tea to help prevent cancer. The skin of the drum is worked so the vibration can travel out to the universe and return.

The colors of the bright, golden, morning sun and the sunset are part of the drum as well. The waters are honored as nurturer, as is the air, which is like breath, and the wind, which is love, warmth, and comfort. The color brown is used to symbolize the Earth, and green is for plants. The Eagle represents the animals. The interaction of the symbols is also significant.

From the time of her birth, the grandmothers of her tribe recognized that Grandmother Rita had the gift of being able to allow spiritual forces to work through her, and she has worked as a healer since she was four years old. "I really still don't know what it is I do, and I don't know after what I did," she explains.

One of the lessons Grandmother Rita learned from her grandmothers was that school was important, but more important was learning about oneself, a principle that has become a cornerstone of her own teachings.

When she was young, Grandmother Rita had diphtheria for two years. "I couldn't speak, all I could do was listen. I could barely breathe."

In 1995, Grandmother Rita discovered she had cancer. By then she knew that in order to be cancer free, she had to heal at even deeper levels. Her cancer was helping her to realize how she had also grown up with anger and then sadness from not having a father.

"My father died a month before I was born," Grandmother Rita explains. "I always wished to have a father to take care of me or hold me, to walk with me. Because I never got to do those things, I had anger as a child. I didn't come here to the planet easily. God told me my life was not going to be easy."

"Our healing is not just for ourselves, it is for the universe."

However, the loss of her father and all she had suffered from were to become the catalysts for her work and her understanding of how to heal and create a better life.

"God said there is only abundance, and the only way through is to forgive. Holding on to negative emotions becomes cancer or another illness. Our healing is not just for ourselves, it is for the universe. We forget who we are, and that is the cause of our illness," Grandmother Rita says.

"It is essential to allow yourself to know what you know, instead of driving yourself to be," she believes. "When there is so much striving to be and become, we don't often recognize what it is we really want when it's right there in front of us."

The elders also taught how important it was not to be just intellectual or full of feelings. Some people just think and don't feel, whereas others feel and don't think. So the thinking never stops, or the feeling never stops, Grandmother Rita says. From a young age, children are taught that when they think of something, they need to also feel it. And when they feel something, they also need to think about it.

"Every one of us in our households growing up were also taught to be polite," Grandmother Rita says. "In our culture, when you don't ask a question, you are being polite. Elders used to tell us to just listen and the answers would come. Maybe one year later, but that's OK. The answer would come when it was needed. It was so ingrained not to interrupt and ask questions that I forget to ask now when somebody is talking to me. But I encourage my young people to ask questions. That's part of learning, I think."

When people come to Grandmother Rita for a healing, she is usually considered their last resort. "The secret is that I don't know anything. All I know is that I am Rita Pitka Blumenstein, I am your friend, I am not sick, not sad, not angry. But what about you?"

With that introduction, Grandmother Rita begins to explore with the patient the emotions that have become the sickness, because she believes that difficult emotions always become illness eventually. "Emotions become physical, and the physical becomes emotional. Healing is about peeling," she says.

Together she and the patient work to peel off the layers of emotions, the hidden disappointments and anger that accumulate from as far back as early childhood, from the roots up. That way together they discover the core emotional problem that is causing the physical problem.

"Physical problems come from all these hidden things, all the disappointments and anger," Grandmother Rita believes. "This happens because we've forgotten who we are."

Grandmother Rita says that it is our need to be perfect that makes us drive ourselves so hard. "We drive ourselves instead of allowing ourselves. We have to hurry, try hard, please somebody, be strong. Those are the drivers. To allow ourselves is to be ourselves. To "do" we need to take

47

our time, consider and respect ourselves, and be open about getting needs met. That's how you become a healer, you know yourself and share it." In fact, Grandmother Rita feels she teaches best by "just being."

People can begin to recognize their gifts through being themselves. "The problem today is that we look too much, we ask too much. We look for answers, but when they come, we don't listen; we don't feel the answers and allow ourselves to really think about the answers," she says.

Grandmother Rita began receiving visions and prophecies when she was nine years old. At first she didn't know what was happening to her. As a protection, her mother cautioned her not to reveal what she was seeing to anyone. But, for Grandmother Rita, it was the hardest job in the world to see and not share. She believes a vision she had of people looking up at the sky in terror turned out to be 9/11.

"We forget who we are, and that is the cause of our illness."

It was her great-grandmother who, more than anyone, trusted what she saw for Grandmother Rita's future as a spiritual leader and healer, when she gave her nine-year-old great-granddaughter the thirteen stones and thirteen eagle feathers that she would one day be passing out at the Grandmothers Council she had seen in her own visions.

Besides her healing work, Grandmother Rita has also taught basket weaving and traditional song and dance in cultural issues classes in more than 150 countries, earning money for Native American colleges. Her teachings about the "Talking Circle" have been published and recorded. As a tribal doctor for the South Central Foundation, Grandmother Rita uses plant and energy medicine to heal, as well as applying the wisdom she learned so long ago from her grandmothers.

In 2006, Grandmother Rita was honored by the mayor and her tribe, when February 18 was declared Rita Pitka Blumenstein Day. Now a widow, Grandmother Rita was happily and peacefully married to a Jewish man for forty-three years. Five of their six children died. "God took them," she says. Her daughter calls herself a "Jewskimo." Rita is a grandmother of six and is training her twelve-year-old granddaughter—who "talks to Mother Earth"—to be a healer and carry on the traditions. On a trip across the country from Seattle to Albany, Grandmother Rita wrote her granddaughter a note to tell her of her tears as she looked down from the plane and felt so sorry for Mother Earth. Everyone seems to feel that they own the land, she told her granddaughter, instead of understanding that the whole universe is for everyone's use. Nothing is to be owned, only shared.

Rita
Pitka
Blumenstein

"Nothing belongs to us," Grandmother Rita says. "We are here for the universe, all of us are here for the universe. Time goes by. Everything changes, except the land we live on. And when that changes, we have to accept it. We can't do anything about it. When Mother Nature shows us She's angry, that changes all of us. My grandmother taught me long ago that you become a human being when you learn to accept, when you learn to let go. We are here for the universe. All of us are here to serve the universe."

Grandmother Rita believes that it was planned a long, long time ago that humanity would be going through thirteen levels of evolution. Though thirteen is most often considered a bad number, Grandmother Rita believes it is a very good number. When she formally introduced herself to the Grandmothers Council, Grandmother Rita had tears in her eyes as she gave each one the special stone and eagle plume given to her by her great-grandmother for the occasion when the Grandmothers finally all met.

"Thirteen stones in honor of the thirteen Grandmothers, the thirteen planets in our universe, and the thirteen full moons of the year," she explained. "We're late, but we're here!"

Inviting the grandmothers to come visit her in Alaska, Grandmother Rita said, "When people think of Alaska they go, 'Brrr.' But I say, when you have a cold heart, that's when you're cold. When you have a warm heart, that's when you are warm. Come to Alaska, and we'll warm you up!"

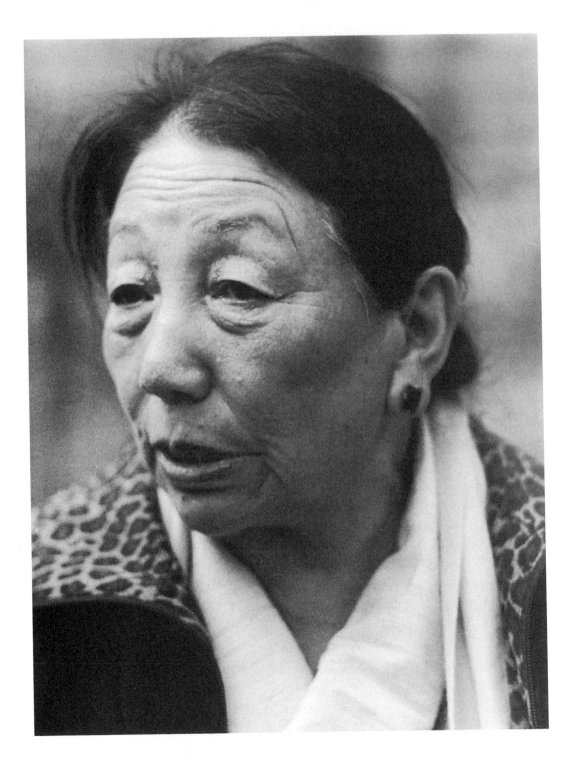

Tsering Dolma Gyaltong
Tibetan Buddhist
(TIBET/CANADA)

IN 1958, with two of her three children strapped to her back and with the eldest left behind in Tibet, Grandmother Tsering Dolma Gyaltong made a treacherous month-long journey through the mountains of her beloved Tibet, to India to escape the brutal Chinese Communist takeover of her homeland. Her husband's work, pleading the Tibetan cause with governments around the world, made it too dangerous for her to remain any longer in her country.

During the Communist takeover, two-thirds of Tibet was absorbed into China, 1.2 million Tibetans were murdered, and 6,254 monasteries and nunneries were destroyed. There was also extensive deforestation of the land. One hundred thousand Tibetans were interred in labor camps, and another one hundred thousand escaped. Grandmother Tsering and her family were forced to make the same journey as the Dalai Lama.

Traveling only during the cover of night to avoid detection made their travels extremely difficult. One night, the horse they had rented stumbled, and Grandmother Tsering's mother and one of her children fell off onto the dark, narrow mountain road. From then on, they all walked while a relative led the horse now carrying only their few provisions.

Grandmother Tsering's oldest child, a daughter, who had been attending a Communist-run school, was left behind with relatives in order to keep her family's flight from being discovered. If she had been suddenly pulled out of the school, the Chinese officials would have been alerted, and most likely all of Grandmother Tsering's family would have been put to death. Like the Dalai Lama, since reaching the safety of India,

Grandmother Tsering and her family have never been able to return to their homeland.

Born in 1933, Grandmother Tsering grew up in the city of Lhasa. There were five children in her family. Three became monks and two, including Grandmother Tsering, stayed at home.

"There has never been great wealth in our family," Grandmother Tsering explains. "But we were a very happy people. Our minds were very happy. We could take care of many children. Many generations lived in one house. Grandparents stayed home and took care of the children while the parents worked."

Grandmother Tsering believes that it is the parents who create the children who grow up and destroy the world. "As the Dalai Lama says," Grandmother Tsering explains, "a child's first teacher is the mother. The mother is the one who teaches them right from wrong and how to be a good person in the culture. Children must be instructed and trained to be kind. They need to be taught to have reverence for life and for spiritual traditions. Such lessons are highly valued in Tibet."

Her grandmother passed away when Grandmother Tsering was twelve. She has a vivid memory of holding her grandmother's hand the moment she died. Afterward, her grandfather continued to live in the family home.

At fifteen, Grandmother Tsering began practicing Buddhism, which taught her that one's individual self is not important, that one's focus needs to be on others, a teaching that sustains her to this day. As she studied, she realized that her grandmother was a wonderful example of someone living to benefit others, and that her mother also had a very positive and generous nature. If someone admired a necklace she was wearing, her mother would take it off and give it to the person without hesitation.

"Women had a difficult time in Tibet," Grandmother Tsering remembers. "I was fortunate, being that I was a girl, to be sent to school. So, in gratitude, I would read and write letters for women who couldn't."

Grandmother Tsering doesn't believe there are many differences among the various spiritual traditions of the world, except that with Buddhism the main teachings are about training the mind.

"Our mind is what we have to be happy within," Grandmother Tsering explains. "If everyone really did a true spiritual practice, which develops a positive mind, the world would not be in the dire situation we find it in today. Even the many wonderful technological advances are not what ultimately make us happy. Within the world, peace has been very difficult to find, and I am disturbed by this lack of peace. Instead of being cared for by the generations within a family, the children go to day care, live outside of the house, and adapt to Western ways. It is difficult for families to stay together now."

Grandmother Tsering is also deeply troubled by the killing and destruction on the planet today. She feels the main reasons for not seeking peace within are the tremendous competition we feel with each other and that individuals hold themselves to be most important.

"People wish for happiness but do not find it. Instead, they find deep suffering and die with deep suffering," she explains. "For example, a person might, through much suffering, gather a great deal of money during their life, but when they die that money isn't going to benefit them. This money that everyone is chasing after does not bring us what we are seeking. Money doesn't bring a person well-being in the end. The real problem is we do not love each other. We do not have this deep pure love that makes the positive connection. There's not enough of that."

Fourteen years after her escape to India, Grandmother Tsering moved with her family to Toronto, Canada. The Dalai Lama and the Tibetan government had asked the people to settle in different countries, and she chose Canada as her refuge. Now Tibetans live in many countries, seeking to bring peace and well-being to wherever they live. Ironically, the message of peace the Tibetan refugees try to bring to the world is lost on the people still living in Tibet. Those left behind have lost their independence and basic human rights. Grandmother Tsering's daily aspiration prayers are for the world and her people to simply know peace and happiness.

Her four grown children all live in Toronto. "I always teach them and make this prayer for them that they benefit all beings in the world, and that their minds are positively motivated, not filled with dark thoughts," she says. "Think always to benefit others and do no harm is what I tell them."

Tsering
Dolma
Gyaltong

On her return to India from Canada in 1984, Grandmother Tsering revived the Tibetan Women's Association, establishing thirty-three branches worldwide, including branches in New York City and Toronto. In 1995, she attended the Fourth World Women's Conference held in Beijing, China, where she faced many threats and dangers as she, along with others, openly criticized the Chinese government for its treatment of the Tibetan people, especially the women of Tibet.

Addressing the Grandmothers for the first time, Grandmother Tsering expressed great hope that the council will help create good human beings, which she believes is what is needed to find peace on Earth. She expressed her belief that it is human beings who create peace on this planet, and human beings who create the suffering. Her belief that today's mothers are creating the mothers of the future and our future is the cornerstone of her work, and she hopes for new discoveries in bringing up children well.

"If everyone really did a true spiritual practice, which develops a positive mind, the world would not be in the dire situation we find it in today."

Grandmother Tsering offered a Tibetan prayer to the council: "Make the spirit of awakening that has not arisen in our hearts arise, and when it arises, may it not diminish but increase."

Mona Polacca

Hopi/Havasupai/Tewa

(ARIZONA)

A MEMBER of the Colorado River Indian tribes that live along the Colorado River in Parker, Arizona, Grandmother Mona believes that giving the origins of her ancestors is as important as telling her name. On her mother's side, she is Havasupai, the people of the blue-green water. The tribal lineage is the Havasupai, who are originally from the Grand Canyon area. On her father's side, she is Hopi-Tewa from the First Mesa in northern Arizona. She is also of the Sun Clan and the Tobacco Clan.

Her last name, Polacca, means butterfly in the Hopi language and is the name received from her paternal grandfather. In Hopi lore, the butterfly is the symbol of man's spiritual transformation.

"At the level of existence, when it crawls on Mother Earth in the form of a caterpillar, it only sees what is right in front of it," Grandmother Mona explains. "Then there comes a time in the development when it puts itself into a little cocoon and enters into darkness. In this darkness, it completely breaks down. During that time a great change takes place."

The Hopi believe that for man, too, this darkness is a prerequisite to experiencing spiritual transformation. Essential to the Hopi mythology is the fact that, though the caterpillar has already become the butterfly in the darkness and can begin to move inside the cocoon and show life again, it does not begin to break out of the cocoon until it is ready.

"Finally, it emerges into this world, into this life as a beautiful creature," Grandmother Mona says. "Yet it doesn't immediately fly away. It sits there as if to be making a connection again with the elements of life: the water, the air, the fire, the earth. Then there is a moment when its wings

start fluttering, developing movement, developing strength within itself using these elements of life. When the moment comes and the butterfly takes flight, it suddenly sees the world from a completely different point of view, a view of vaster beauty and a much, much wider worldview. This is what I was told about being a butterfly."

Grandmother Mona learned the Indian ways of being in the world from her father's mother, who lived to be 102. "She was a praying lady," Grandmother Mona says. "She would always talk to me about how to be a good person. Be kind. Be nice to one another. Love your brothers and sisters, they are all you have. She'd say, 'In Indian way, this is the way to be, this is the way to do things.'"

Grandmother Mona never knew her mother's mother, who was Havasupai. All she has is a photograph of her that hangs in the doorway of her home.

"As I go out the doorway of my home," Grandmother Mona says, "I receive the blessing of my grandmother looking at me. I tell her I am going to be away from here for a while, look after this home for me. When I come back into my home, I receive the welcome of my grandmother looking at me. Though I've never met her, I have this connection with her."

Grandmother Mona's maternal grandfather and great-grandfather were the last chiefs of the Havasupai Nation. Through the prayers of her ancestors, elders, and different relatives, Grandmother Mona believes the Creator has made a way for her in this world, and she has, in fact, been put on a specific path by their prayers. She has always known that prayers for her life were begun way, way before she was born. Grandparents many generations back prayed for the generations to come.

"They prayed for the great-great-great-great-grandchildren they would never see, but that they knew were life coming. They prayed for us to be praying people, to continue the prayer, and to recognize through a prayer when you are blessed. The way I have been taught in walking this road is to always take time to acknowledge our ancestors, those who were here before us and were the ones who made the prayers that made it possible for us to be here. In order for me to be able to stand or kneel on Mother Earth, to make a prayer, it's because of them."

For Grandmother Mona, these prayers are like an arrowhead that moves in front of her, making a way, clearing a path, and she just walks behind it. "I try to look at whatever comes along in a day as part of the blessing from that ancient prayer," she says.

The teaching that she carries with her everywhere was given to her by her mother. "She said, 'You are not here just for yourself. Wherever you go, you are a representative of our family: mother, father, grandparents, aunts, uncles, everyone. You represent our tribe, our people. So when you go somewhere, that's who you are—our representative.'"

As a result, Grandmother Mona takes great care in her speech and with her actions, while her work has taken her to many places in the world. She travels for her mother as well, since her mother will never have such opportunities. "Bring me back a little something," her mother always tells Grandmother Mona. "A small stone or shell. Something simple like that."

For nearly thirty years, Grandmother Mona has worked in the field of alcoholism and substance abuse. From the beginning, she was told by her grandmother and her parents to pray for those who suffer and to be kind to them. By being treated kindly, someday it will click, and they will recognize that they are worthy, someone who has something to offer.

"It doesn't take a lot to make a kind gesture to someone, regardless of how bad off they are," Grandmother Mona says. "If a homeless person walks up to me, I will always give them a few coins, because I know I have a brother who could be homeless and not having anything to eat, not even a cup of coffee. When they walk away, I say a prayer for them. I try to extend that kindness to them, so that somewhere along the way they will be able to have a good life again, be all right."

"I try to look at whatever comes along in a day as part of the blessing from an ancient prayer."

Initially during the early 1970s, when the first federally funded social programs to aid the Native Americans were brought to the reservations, Grandmother Mona focused on alcoholism and drug-addiction prevention and working with the youth. Many of the tribes were hiring experts from outside the community, and Grandmother Mona began questioning the necessity of these outside experts, feeling all the resources they needed were right there on the reservation.

"Well, my questions were turned around on me," she says, "and I was given the job to develop programs for our youth."

Grandmother Mona organized youth and elder conferences that were held in the winter and the spring, where elders of the tribe would talk to young people about life and the traditional ways. The young people were able to hear traditional songs sung properly and learn traditional games, which gave them a greater sense of identity, purpose, and direction. A fire would be built on the grounds, where celebrations were held, and prayers would be offered by the elders.

"Once, a Mohave elder stood by the fire, looked around at everyone before he offered his prayer and said, 'You know, there is really something special about this. Nonnatives so often build a huge bonfire, so big that everyone has to stand back. Natives build a small fire, so that everyone has to come closer.' That was the way we worked, all close around the fire, so that we could all hear each other and feel the warmth, too."

The young people became involved in the running of the conferences. Some cooked the meals, and all ate together, because to natives food is considered a spiritual part of life, capable of nurturing the spirit as well as the physical body.

"We were exposing the young people to the spirituality in everyday life," Grandmother Mona explains. "Most of these elders are gone now, but I still try to work this way wherever I go. The youth learn these ways are accessible, not meant to be just seen under glass in a museum, where you can only stand and look. Their hands can hold the traditional sacred ways. It's not just our history, but an essential part of our life today."

When people who are deeply into alcoholism can set aside their addiction and choose to become productive people, deciding their life is worth living, Grandmother Mona is gratified. She sees how the community is positively affected, especially when one who is healed reaches his or her hand back to help others.

Grandmother Mona has been involved in several studies of addictive behavior. One study revealed that the primary motivation for Native American women to overcome substance abuse is the threat of their children being taken away. Another study of youth proved her instincts to be correct, that young people responded positively to programs with a cultural component, like sweat lodges, singing, and drumming. Given a deep level of connection with who they were—with their tribes, ancestors, and their traditional symbols—was the one element that created progress. Even if far from their reservations, those who maintain a close connection with the ceremonies, which give respect for self and for sacred ways of living, are able to maintain their sobriety.

Grandmother Mona, who has a son, two daughters, and seven grandchildren, addressed the Grandmothers of the council as "beautiful relatives of the world." She explained that the Hopi way when meeting those of other nations is to reach out an open hand to show one has come in peace. She also paid honor to Grandfather Fire, represented by the fire lit from the original flame of peace.

"There was once a time as indigenous people when we didn't have any maps or road signs, yet we were able to make our way. We were able to journey," Grandmother Mona explained. "We had the sacred fire, so that when there was a moment when we felt we lost our sense of direction, when we were lost and disoriented, not knowing which direction to go, we would sit down before this Grandpa Fire. In poor health physically, mentally, spiritually, we would sit down before Grandpa Fire and say our prayers. In that way we would be shown the direction we needed to go, the things we needed to do. We would be given the signs through Grandfather Fire. Our hearts would be filled with warmth, love, and compassion. That's the way this Grandfather Fire is. Always respect it, always look to it, let it be there to help you.

"This teaching about Grandpa Fire was given to me by my mother, so that I could sit here with the Grandmothers who all came here with good feeling, seeking something good and a new direction, not only for ourselves but for all of the people," she said.

Rita Long Visitor Holy Dance
Beatrice Long Visitor Holy Dance

Oglala Lakota

(SOUTH DAKOTA)

SISTERS Rita and Beatrice Long Visitor Holy Dance, descendants of Long Visitor, are members of the Crazy Horse Band, named after one of the most revered Oglala Lakota Indian warriors. Crazy Horse fought fiercely to prevent American encroachment on Lakota lands and to preserve his people's traditional way of life. They are from the southwest corner of the Pine Ridge Reservation of southwestern South Dakota, considered the place of the most overwhelming poverty in America. There is no commercial activity on the reservation except a couple of gas stations, a Pizza Hut, Taco John's, and a grocery-hardware store. Unemployment is 85 percent.

The Oglala Lakota of the Pine Ridge Reservation are the largest band of the great Sioux Nation, representing the majority of the Teton Sioux. Since 1890, when their main sustenance of life, the huge herds of buffalo, were decimated for sport by the nonnative settlers, the Lakota have been reduced to chronic conditions of poverty, poor health, and despair. To some, the violence, drunkenness, the 45 to 62 percent school dropout rate, and a suicide rate that is twice the national average seem to serve the United States government in its continuing efforts to purchase the Black Hills.

In 1868, the United States had actually set aside the Black Hills for the Lakota in the Fort Laramie Treaty, but a year later gold was discovered, and Congress grabbed the land rights back. In 1980, a United States

Rita Long Visitor Holy Dance

Supreme Court opinion was handed down stating that "the taking of the Black Hills (sixty billion dollars in gold) is the most ripe and rank case of dishonorable dealing ever perpetrated on a people by the United States government."

Yet despite being the poorest of the poor, 90 percent of the Lakota people still steadfastly refuse the United States government's offer of a half billion dollars to buy their sacred Black Hills. They do not consider themselves to be poor, ignorant, heathen savages, but a people with a different set of values. To the Lakota, land, air, and water cannot be thought of in terms of dollars and cents. Such a purchase would mean a sellout of the Lakota nation, culture, and religion.

The Black Hills have been the center of the Lakota's world for over five hundred years and have been known to nonnatives for only a couple of hundred. The Black Hills were deemed a holy place. Now, many sites where their ancestors prayed have been desecrated.

Many different kinds of plant medicines grow in the Black Hills. Traditionally, a person with a gift for healing would say prayers, and then a gift of tobacco and red willow would be given to the Earth and the specific plant at a specific time of the year, before the medicine man or woman would decide what part of the plant was to be used for the healing. Would only the leaves be needed? Or the stem? If the root was needed, were there enough other plants to ensure the species' survival for the next seven generations?

Grandmothers Rita and Beatrice remember having a good life growing up, despite the fact that their home was heated only by wood and lit by kerosene lamps. Grandmother Beatrice hauled water from the river to their house until 1985, when she finally had running water installed. Food was provided by the garden at the bottom of the hill. In years gone by, at harvest time, the women of the community would come together to help each other and to dry the corn. The sisters burst into gales of laughter as they recall, as young women, racing up the steep hill carrying huge squash in sacks on their backs or a canvas full of beans. Everything was done by hand. The family also had a lot of cattle and chickens.

When, at seven, Rita went off to the Catholic school in the family wagon, five-year-old Beatrice wept and wept.

Beatrice Long Visitor Holy Dance

"I was sent to school with new moccasins and a shawl," Grandmother Rita recalls. "I didn't know a word of English. When I arrived, the nuns grabbed my hand and took me from one place to another. I didn't understand anything they were saying. We went down one hall and then another, where I heard children screaming and playing. The nuns opened a door onto a great big playroom, where there were little girls playing. That's where I had to stay until they gave me a bed."

The next day, Rita attended school. She didn't understand a word the teacher was saying and just sat there. "After weeks and months went by," Grandmother Rita says, "I began to understand the language, especially 'yes' and 'no'! That was kind of hard. My own Lakota language was finally cut out of my mind, because we would get punished if we ever spoke it."

Children spent nine months out of the year boarding at the school, and the other three were spent helping at home. When Beatrice was old enough, she also went to this boarding school. She remembers that she and Rita always got into a lot of mischief together, whether in school or at home. They were natural pranksters.

"I always appreciated what the nuns did for me at the school," Grandmother Beatrice says. "They would put away the clothes we came in and furnish us with new clothing, new shoes. The nuns and priests taught us a lot of good things, from what I can recall. We were taught how to work in different areas of the school: the kitchen, dormitories, dining rooms. They showed us what to do and how to do it. And it was good. We got up at six, went to mass every morning at seven, and then to school. It was our home for nine months out of the year."

Grandmother Beatrice recalls how a Catholic brother from Switzerland grew the food in the garden. In the fall, when the children returned to school, he and the boys harvested the garden. "There was a root cellar, where they took all the vegetables from the garden for storage," she recalls. "This brother would make barrels and barrels of sauerkraut and dill pickles for the kids. One nun took care of the milk and made butter. Another brother was in charge of the bakery with the boys. There were chickens and cattle. We ate meat, chicken, eggs, whatever we wanted. Everything was fresh every day. We all learned to wash dishes, clean the tables, and help with the cooking."

Life continued this way, until 1942, when their mother became sick with cancer. After graduating from eighth grade, Rita had to stay home for four years. She had to help her father as well as her mother, because he was a Tribal Council representative and needed her help with the cattle and horses. Beatrice was able to go back to school with her brothers. Finally, their mother, Antonia Long Visitor Holy Dance, was bedridden for nine months. She passed away in 1946.

"It was a sad time for us," Grandmother Rita remembers. "For almost a month, our dad spent his nights at the cemetery. In the beginning, I would wonder where he was and finally learned he was sleeping at her grave. We had a good dad. We always had everything we needed. Our dad never let us go hungry after we left school. He made sure we had clothing. He even took care of us after we married. He didn't have to, but he did."

"We must reach our grandchildren. They need to understand that the Creator provides all that we need."

Once they left school, Rita and Beatrice worked in the potato fields, which was hard physical labor. They had to stay in a tent during the harvest time. Beatrice was the cook. Rita was in the fields, where she earned three cents for every bushel of potatoes picked, which weighed about a hundred pounds.

"That's what I worked for then. I paid Beatrice a penny to clean my potatoes," Grandmother Rita recalls, giggling. "We'd go downtown and never buy anything, but we would buy books. Sometimes twenty at a time. That was when we were young. Of course, we had to have a double wedding. I couldn't get married unless Beatrice did. So she had to. Dad provided the wedding dinner, a double wedding dinner!"

Grandmother Rita was married four years before she had children, and Grandmother Beatrice already had four herself. "People made fun of me," Grandmother Rita recalls. "They said I was taking bad medicine so that I wouldn't have children. My feelings were hurt. I helped Beatrice take care of her children, and I prayed to the Great Spirit, why didn't I have children? Then I had all these kids, including twins, seven boys and finally one girl."

As the years passed and they had their families, Rita and Beatrice hardly ever saw each other. Rita became isolated from having so many sons, because having daughters was what involved the women in community life. In 1971, Rita left the reservation to seek employment and provide a better economic situation for her children.

Nineteen years after their mother passed away, their father died as a result of a car accident. Since then, the sisters hold their parents and grandparents in their prayers every night and every morning. During the days of preparing food for sacred ceremonies, they pray for their parents. Many tears are shed then, remembering their loved ones.

"Now I have a three-bedroom home," Grandmother Beatrice says. "I don't have much. I have running water, but it isn't very good. I have mold growing there, and it's getting pretty bad. I've been trying to get the housing authority to help me, but nobody helps me."

Grandmother Beatrice continues her work with the field health nurses seven days a week, four to six hours a day, delivering medication to TB patients. Before then, she worked as a community health representative, working with diabetics. Originally she had wanted to be a nurse, but wasn't given the opportunity.

"I work with a lot of sick people who don't understand what the doctors are telling them, about how they are supposed to diet and take care of themselves," Grandmother Beatrice says. "I've worked in the health fields since 1974, trying to help our people. They're really poor, having a hard time. Some are worse off than we are."

Grandmother Beatrice feels they shouldn't be taking so many pills, that her people need to return to herbal medicine, that she should as well, despite her extensive heart trouble, which she regrets was caused by smoking.

Grandmothers Rita and Beatrice are extremely concerned not only about the poverty on the reservation but also about the enormous problem of alcohol and drug abuse. Alcohol has robbed their families of children. The sisters lost their oldest and youngest brothers and two grandchildren to the disease.

"Our Lakota people didn't know alcohol," Grandmother Beatrice explains. "They were clean. They ate well and lived well. Alcohol was brought into this country. Now it's destroying our people, destroying all the tribes all over the nation. They don't know how to handle it. Even

67

worse are all the drugs these days. We must reach our grandchildren. They need to understand that the Creator provides all that we need. He takes care of us. They don't have to use the alcohol."

Grandmother Beatrice recalls that the situation was not like it is now when they were growing up. Now, when young boys ask their grandmothers for money, mostly for drugs, the boys treat their grandmothers poorly if they don't get the money. Young people, thirteen and fourteen years old, are having babies. Men and women are passed out on the sidewalks. Some beg for money and are threatening if they don't get it. The sisters say such behavior is all about trying to survive in a hostile world.

"It's really, really bad," Grandmother Beatrice says. "We are Sun Dancing and praying for our people. We pray that the alcoholism, drugs, and illegal activities leave the younger generation alone. I keep telling them that the evil spirit is going after them and controlling them. It gets inside of you and won't let you go. Try to get it out of your system, I tell them. Go home to your family who loves you, who doesn't want to see you like this. I tell them that. You have to be gentle with them, and then they always thank me. But it is dangerous to go to town. I take Rita with me."

"I'm her bouncer!" Grandmother Rita laughs and then grows serious. "We use Indian medicine all the time at home. Our spiritual ways, our Sun Dance ways are encouraging prayer and bringing a lot of people back. A lot of young boys and girls are coming into the Sun Dance and are learning to reconnect with the source of their being."

The Lakota have seven rites within their tradition that legend says was given to them by White Buffalo Calf Woman nineteen generations ago: the Keeping of the Soul, the Rite of Purification, Crying for a Vision, the Sun Dance, the Making of Relatives, Preparing a Girl for Womanhood, and Throwing of the Ball.

Addressing the Grandmothers Council, Grandmothers Beatrice and Rita spoke of their gratitude at being asked to join with the Grandmothers in speaking about peace, love, hope, faith, and charity, all the things that go with our Mother Earth. They hope that their work on the council will bring many good things for the children, grandchildren, and all the children to come, and also will give a voice to the Lakota people.

Maria Alice Campos Freire
Santo Daime
(AMAZON RAIN FOREST OF BRAZIL)

WHEN GRANDMOTHER MARIA ALICE was a little girl, she found it very difficult to live on the Earth. "I couldn't fit into the structures and felt very far away from the reality here," she explains. "I had a greater connection with the stars and the Star Beings who showed me many things."

Her mind was full of memories that were very different from life on Earth. "I was sure I was very old," she says. "Now that I am a grand-mother, I feel like a child!"

No one in her family understood her. "They were very good people," she explains. "They were concerned with political and social questions but were also very materialistic. They weren't at all spiritual."

Grandmother Maria Alice was named after her father's mother, whom everyone considered crazy, because she developed memory prob-lems and seemed to live in another world. The only thing she remem-bered was how to play the piano and sing. Still, Grandmother Maria Alice remembers her grandmother as happy, and she loved the children.

Her other grandmother passed away when Maria Alice's own mother was a young girl, but her life impacted Maria Alice's nevertheless. "I heard a lot about her," Grandmother Maria Alice says. "She was some-one who took care of everybody. She died because she was taking care of so many people during a measles epidemic that she had no time to take care of herself. She left five children. My mother went to live with her grandmother afterward. My great-grandmother was a very poor woman who prayed all the time.

"All of my grandmothers lived on another level," Grandmother Maria Alice explains. "And this is what I am also. I live more on those levels, too. I live much more with lots of Grandmothers on the other side. This is my life. I work with spiritual guides and spirits. These Grandmothers, who are not present in this world but are my spiritual group, are a very strong influence in my life."

Growing up in Brazil, Grandmother Maria Alice was subjected to war and persecution. When she was seventeen, she was imprisoned and tortured while living in Chile. During her imprisonment, she was pregnant with her daughter. Her daughter was born after Maria Alice was received as a political refugee in Europe. Grandmother Maria Alice sought help when her daughter was crying all the time, and she was advised to move to Africa. Immediately upon arriving there, her daughter never again cried, and Grandmother Maria Alice began to awaken and surrender to her spirituality. She was twenty-three. While in Africa, she received many instructions for her future and had her first experiences connecting with past lives.

After receiving amnesty, Grandmother Maria Alice returned to Brazil, where new doors opened for her. She had her initiation in Umbanda, a Brazilian syncretic religion, based on African, Brazilian, indigenous, and Christian traditions. In one Umbanda ritual, a black man appeared in a vision. He was an extremely enlightened being from the Universe. The man gave her messages signed with the name "Mestre (Master) Irineu."

She came to learn that Master Irineu was the spiritual guardian of a sacramental tea named Santo Daime. When he had lived on the Earth, his name was Raimundo Irineu Serra. He was seven feet tall. Born on the northeast coast of Brazil, he moved to the Amazon as an adult and worked as a rubber tapper. One day he was offered a tea made from two power plants of the forest: the vine Mariri and the leaf Chacrona. This was Ayahuasca, the sacramental tea of the ancient indigenous people of the Amazon. In a vision, he met the "Queen of the Forest," a white woman dressed in blue, whom he took to be the Virgin Mary. The woman instructed him to found a new religion using this sacramental entheogenic tea in special rituals, presenting Christian doctrine with special songs and dances. *Santo Daime* means "holy give me herb," which is an appeal to be given divine illumination and healing. The tea is brewed by boiling the divine plants, creating a pathway for the teachings to come through.

Just after Grandmother Maria Alice's vision of Master Irineu, she was offered the opportunity to drink Santo Daime, which was a new step in her spiritual initiation. During the initiation, she was instructed to go to the Amazon, where she was told she would discover the other important facet of her spiritual origins. She was to become a blend of Brazilian, Native, African, and Christian spirituality.

"I began to open my understanding," Grandmother Maria Alice explains. "Now I saw I needed that big suffering to awaken to my spirituality. This was my challenge."

In the Amazon, she met Padrinho Sebastião, a disciple of Master Irineu and leader of a spiritual community deep in the Amazon rain forest. He had called to her in spirit. When Grandmother Maria Alice didn't have the money it would take to go to where he lived, a friend gave her all she needed, and she and her two daughters traveled in complete trust to the remote forest. The government had set aside the land as a reservation, and Sebastião's community was given the job of taking care of it. When she arrived, Sebastião welcomed her as if she were his daughter.

Many people came from all over the world to visit Sebastião and his community, and to drink the holy medicine in order to connect with their past lives and to understand their present task in the world. Santo Daime, like peyote and the medicines of many other indigenous peoples around the world, is used only for spiritual purposes and within the context of ceremony and ritual. With this medicine, people are able to clearly see what it is psychologically that blocks them from being who they really are. Community life is greatly enhanced by its use, and the overall benefits are considered to be remarkable. In addition, there are no addictions, nor any characteristic behaviors associated with drug abuse.

"We came to the forest to live a more real life, a more truthful life."

The community practices traditional medicine, using all the sacred plants of the Amazon for healing. Grandmother Maria Alice feels graced

72

from the purity of the beings of the forest, the trees, the plants, and the mushrooms. "Humans have so much to clean out psychologically to match the peace and beauty of the forest," she says. "Our community is dedicated to bringing this level of happiness to people, to show that such joy is possible. We are happy, because we are devoted.

Maria Alice Campos Freire

"I had a vision, was guided, and have surrendered seventeen years of my life to this community," Grandmother Maria Alice continues. "It is a big challenge to be in a spiritual community in the middle of the jungle. If you want to run away, it's not possible. This was a conscious decision to live here, and to keep the commitment."

Grandmother Maria Alice is grateful that she surrendered to her destiny. The community has grown to one thousand members. At spiritual festivals, as many as eighteen hundred are singing and dancing to God, which is why Grandmother Maria Alice feels the people are so happy.

"We came to the forest to live a more real life, a more truthful life," Grandmother Maria Alice explains. "That comes from working with the land and respecting nature. Planting seeds, harvesting, finding the wood for our fires is not easy and can create many hardships, but the struggle is what ultimately makes us happy. Being in this forest has finally made me happy to live on the Earth. I am so grateful to be able to live in harmony with all the creatures and talk with the plants and clouds and rivers. And then to share this with others and live in this healing process with all of nature; I feel blessed."

Also part of the Santo Daime community is Clara Shinobu Iura, a member of the Grandmothers Council. Grandmother Clara arrived within months of Grandmother Maria Alice. Sebastião saw exceptional healing powers in both women that they found difficult to see themselves and always had them do their healing work together. Since 1998, they have traveled the world helping other communities and their churches in their healing work.

"Fate has kept Clara and I together," Grandmother Maria Alice believes. "Whenever it seems we are moving in different directions, something comes up and we are drawn together again."

At the moment of the highly revered Sebastião's passing, his son put one of his father's hands in Grandmother Clara's and one in Grandmother

Maria Alice's. For both women, who felt humble to be so honored, it was a profoundly sacred moment.

Grandmother Maria Alice is a Madrinha of the Umbanda ceremonies in the Santo Daime Church in Ceu do Mapia. She is also a healer with the Amazonian plant medicines, founder of the Centro Medicina da Floresta, and an activist for the preservation of the indigenous rain forest heritage. She is extremely grateful that she was inspired by her spiritual master and received from him the mission to make a legal organization to safeguard the medicine of the Amazon. She is also dedicated to the education of children and young people, as the main way of continuing her work and keeping traditional knowledge for all time.

The Amazon, Earth's greatest biological treasure, once covered 14 percent of the Earth's surface and now covers only 6 percent. The last remaining rain forests could be consumed in less than forty years. Nearly half the world's species of plants, animals, and microorganisms will then be destroyed or severely threatened, the result of deforestation by multinational corporations and landowners.

Lost will be many possible cures for life-threatening diseases. Five centuries ago, ten million Indians lived in the Amazon rain forest. The conquistadores, who came with a cross in one hand and a sword in the other, killed many indigenous peoples and made millions slaves. Today, there are less than two hundred thousand Indians left. Gone are thousands of years of irreplaceable knowledge about the medicinal properties of the plants. It is said that each time a shaman or medicine person dies, it is as if a whole library is burning down.

As pharmaceutical companies discover the extraordinary value of the rain-forest plants for healing many illnesses, including cancer, they are now scrambling to preserve what they can, Grandmother Maria Alice says. Their understanding is still narrow and biased. For instance, there is no understanding that incorporating the plant's properties in a pill is far less effective than using the plant in its natural state, as the life force of the plant, an essential element in healing, is destroyed in pill form.

Addressing the Grandmothers Council for the first time, Grandmother Maria Alice spoke of what a very special moment it was for her to be there with all of them. "I believe we have all been guided to be here," she said. "And we will be guided to do what we came here to do. We cannot say we are of this race or that one. We have all been everything in our many lives, and now our paths cross for us to connect from many different faiths and cultures. But we are all the same flame in life.

Maria Alice Campos Freire

"I am thankful for this holy Mother, our planet the Earth, who received all of us, for the destiny we have here to be this channel for eternal life in receiving the knowledge from our ancestors to give to future generations."

Grandmother Maria Alice believes all of the Grandmothers on the council have experienced much to be a part of the council. "We have all arrived at the point where we are very sure about what is good for us, what is good for humanity. Although we may not know many things, we have this force and certainty about what is good for all of us humans. We know we don't need violence, money, struggle, or competition. We just need to surrender and consecrate God's Creation. We need to be happy, love one another, and receive what God has to give us.

"Although we are old ones, our voice is very important for the world at this moment. The misunderstanding in this world is that some men think they are very big. We are small ones with this love, which is the only big thing we have. We can give good words for the world. I have a very big faith that we are able to change something, that we are going to be able to give hope for our next generations."

Clara Shinobu Iura

Santo Daime

(AMAZON RAIN FOREST OF BRAZIL)

THE DAUGHTER of Japanese immigrants, Grandmother Clara Shinobu Iura was born in a city in the interior of the state of São Paulo and raised in São Paulo Capital, Brazil.

"I was the kind of person who did not believe in spiritual truths," says Grandmother Clara. "I studied pure philosophy and was fascinated by epistemology, the theory of knowledge."

Her family's religious lineage was traditional Buddhism, and her great-grandmother was one of the first women in Japan to have access to sacred scriptures, which left an indelible impression on her heart.

According to stories told by Clara's mother, the door of the monastery was open during meals to feed the indigent, as they were respected as a very special class of people in Japan. "The rules of the scriptures stated that the monks were to eat the same meals at the same table as the indigent people," Grandmother Clara explains. "But, with time, these rules were broken, and the monks began to eat special foods in a separate place. But my great-grandmother did not change her custom of eating with the poor. This story made me happy and proud to have been descended from a woman of integrity, a defender of the sacred principles, someone who anticipated liberty despite her condition as a woman in the nineteenth century," she says.

Grandmother Clara recalls that from childhood she was already a bit different, tending to question why things are the way they are and very concerned with social injustices and differences. She did not feel at ease within the Japanese community, which was very repressive, especially toward women. They were very concerned with appearances so as not to shame the Japanese race, which had lost World War II.

At a time when Brazilian politics were in upheaval, something happened that set Grandmother Clara's heart free: her father, who had a chain of furniture stores, went bankrupt. Her family, now broke, was discredited. No longer a young woman of privilege, Grandmother Clara was allowed to work, and work gave her freedom to "be," to lead a true life without being accountable to the Japanese community.

"After that experience, I began a search to understand the essence of existence—who am I, why I was born to my family, and what is the foundation of the truth of life? At that time, I believed that everything, even God, could be a creation of the mind," Grandmother Clara explains.

Grandmother Clara then decided to study philosophy, believing that it and books could provide the answers she was looking for. Around 1968, she joined the rapidly emerging social liberation movements that were contesting the dominant status quo. It was a time of searching and indignation on the part of youth and people who believed in social justice.

"During this time, I experienced many things that led me finally to extreme consequences," Grandmother Clara recalls. "When I finally awoke and realized my situation, I was carrying a sack of clothing and living in an abandoned house cooking out of a can. Fortunately, I was saved by Divine Providence, when I was magically put in touch with people of different faiths and spiritual teachings. Through them, I received a spiritual initiation and was finally able to leave the dark universe where my searching had taken me."

Grandmother Clara cannot forget the people connected to Bagwan Rajneesh, who, through his system and disciples, opened the doors of her perception, making space for a sacred universe she had never before imagined could be a part of her life. Things that she'd believed were a fictional creation of the mind began showing themselves to her as true facts. She began to live with the unknown, and the most varied types of spirits came to talk with her and give her proof of what they were saying. They brought her much knowledge and many inner transformations.

Most remarkable was a three-month-long encounter with beings who told Grandmother Clara that they were from another planet, one of an incalculable distance away from Earth. They had come to make contact and to leave a message with the people of planet Earth. They spoke in a strange language, using her body as a receiver. "I'd never experienced anything like it," she says. "After a while, those strange words seemed to find a mechanism in my own body that permitted a translation into our language in a way that wouldn't allow my mind to interfere. I heard words that before, as a philosophy student with Marxist tendencies, I would not dare to pronounce: totality of the universe, planet Earth, millions of light years, et cetera, words that reminded me of *Flash Gordon* or something similar, even though I never read science fiction. When they entered in contact with me, I felt my body alter, and during those three months I almost did not sleep or eat. Everything happened fantastically. I could not doubt it because the evidence was great."

Clara Shinobu Iura

The beings left a message to the people of Earth, an alert telling us not to lose ourselves in our material and technological lives, not to forget our spiritual consciousness, not to forget God the great spirit-creator of all things, Grandmother Clara says. "They told us to stop disrespecting His creation and to stop the destruction of our planet, which is resulting in the sickness of the Earth and her inhabitants. They told us that this destruction would continue, and that only a change to spiritual consciousness would give hope for our salvation. They warned us that it is necessary to be attentive to products created by technology that can pollute and destroy our terrestrial atmosphere. They said that it was necessary to enter into a state of alert. This was twenty-eight years ago, when these questions were not yet so grave."

The beings also told Grandmother Clara that she was destined, along with many other conscious people worried about the same issues, to take this message to all the inhabitants of Earth before the grand catastrophe that would bring much destruction and disgrace to all humanity, something already prophesied by peoples with sacred knowledge. During this same period of contact, they said that soon Grandmother

Clara would meet people in a location between Rio and São Paulo, who were in search of spiritual consciousness and were preoccupied with the preservation of nature.

"At the time, I was very confused and thought that all this would happen immediately," Grandmother Clara says. "I was even alarmed. But nothing happened. I was about to give up and store this cosmic experience in a drawer in my memory, forgetting what I was told. But it all came back when I encountered Santo Daime in the mountains of Visconde de Mauá, between Rio and São Paulo. It was then that I had my first contact with the sacred drink and the hymns sung during the sacrament, which invoked spiritual consciousness, praised the sun, moon and stars, the forest, the earth and the sea. These were the people for whom I'd been searching for over seven years."

The people who introduced her to Santo Daime lived communally. The leader of the doctrine, Sebastião Mota de Melo, lived in the depths of the Amazon forest. Clara met him in Rio de Janeiro where he'd come for health treatments. Upon visiting him, to her great surprise Sebastião exclaimed, "Ah! Finally the person they (the spirits) said they would send to cure me has arrived." He didn't know Grandmother Clara, and it was the first time he saw her.

"I was the kind of person who did not believe in spiritual truths. I studied pure philosophy and was fascinated by epistemology, the theory of knowledge."

From then on, doors opened and brought her to Céu to Mapiá, in the Amazon forest where she still lives, invited by Padrinho Sabastião to help him.

Despite having accepted the invitation, Grandmother Clara was profoundly uneasy. How could a person so highly regarded for his wisdom trust her, a sinner subject to so many errors and so ignorant? There were many times when she distrusted him. At the same time, she admired his courage to found a community, in the middle of the forest distant from everything, in order to create a true doctrine, with the hopes of raising the banner of a new world, with a new system of natural and healthy living, turned toward God, and far from a world polluted by lies and illusions that distance us from our true Self.

"Sebastião encouraged everyone to search for God within themselves," Grandmother Clara explains. "He encouraged all to be and not to 'appear to be,' and to spread the divine truth of our Mother Nature to all the people of the Earth. He was amazing in all his simplicity and incredibly strong when pronouncing divine truth."

Today, almost eighteen years after her arrival in the Amazon forest, which she never again left, Grandmother Clara feels she is a testimony to the truth of the spiritual path she has chosen. Becoming a member of the Council of Grandmothers and becoming a voice praying for the Earth—with the quest that humanity becomes more conscious of the planet on which we live and of the spiritual truth of our being—have become her cause. She teaches of the necessity for each native nation living on Mother Earth to preserve the wisdom received from God and to preserve this wisdom for future generations. "It is my hope that, with the love and care of a grandmother, the words of our Council will enter the hearts of the men who govern this Earth," Grandmother Clara says, "and awaken the child who inhabits each of them, so that their spiritual consciousness will be illuminated, thus reversing the course of history."

Aama Bombo (Buddhi Maya Lama)
Tamang
(NEPAL)

BUDDHI MAYA LAMA, who is also known as Aama Bombo (Mother Shaman), was born into a poor family in the remote village of Melong in the eastern part of the Bagmati zone, Nepal. Her father was a renowned shaman, and her mother the second of his seven wives. There were nine children altogether.

Life was a struggle for Grandmother Aama while growing up. Her mother eloped when Aama was ten, leaving Aama to be raised by her grandmother. In the Tamang tradition into which Grandmother Aama was born, whose ancestry is Tibetan and comprises the largest ethnic group in Nepal, women were not permitted to practice shamanism. Despite the fact that she had wanted to be a healer since she was five years old, Aama was restricted by her father in every way from developing her gifts. When she was sixteen, Aama moved to Katmandu, where she fell in love with and married a man who had two wives. They all lived in harmony in one household. Grandmother Aama's father died at the age of eighty.

WHEN SHE WAS TWENTY-FIVE, Grandmother Aama began to have unusual sensations of shaking in her body, a condition that lasted for the next fourteen months. The people around her believed she was becoming mentally ill and took her to many healers, seeking a cure, but to no avail. The only course seemed to be for her to be admitted to a psychiatric hospital.

But, as a last resort, Grandmother Aama was taken to a Buddhist lama, who was able to uncover the problem. Apparently, in the nine years since his death, her father's spirit had been seeking someone through whom he could transmit his teachings and pass on his work. But he could not find anyone with a good enough heart, and he had to accept that only Grandmother Aama was pure enough to transmit his teachings, even though she was a female. When Grandmother Aama was able to recognize and honor his and other spirits that wanted to work through her, she began to feel better. Since then, all of her knowledge of shamanic healing has come to her through her father and the gods and spirits that began visiting her and teaching her their healing ways.

"I am doing my prayers around the world to create a world without war and tension."

Grandmother Aama is now a beloved and well-known shaman in Nepal. She treats the poorest of the poor, as well as members of the royal family, including the king, with equal dedication and respect. She begins her day at four in the morning with prayers at the temple to the god Shiva, the destroyer who dissolves in order to create. She often walks as she prays. People begin arriving at her home by six, and the healing goes on until noon. After a short rest, she resumes her work. Grandmother Aama can easily see a hundred people a day. As well as coming from all over Nepal, many also travel from India and Tibet to seek her help for all kinds of physical, emotional, and spiritual problems for themselves and for their children. She gives healings, cleans their homes of negative energy, and guides them. She also teaches. The guidance she has given to all the members of the royal family has come to pass, including her prediction of the massacre that ended their royal line. She worked a great deal with the late king.

When she is doing her healing work, Grandmother Aama calls on her father's spirit first, then the spirits of her clan, followed by the nature spirits of her surroundings, and then the gods and goddesses from the four directions and from the sky, the land, the waters, the above world, and the underworld. Kali, the dark, fearless mother, is to Grandmother Aama her most important deity, but the Monkey god, Hanuman-ji, is also vital to her healing work. Hanuman-ji is the mighty ape

84

that aided Lord Rama in his expedition against the evil forces and is one of the most popular deities in the Hindu pantheon. Believed to be the avatar of Lord Shiva and disciple of Lord Rama, he is worshipped for his physical strength, perseverance, and devotion and teaches devotees about the unlimited power that lies unused in each of us. Grandmother Aama channels all of these spirits and deities.

Aama Bombo (Buddhi Maya Lama)

She is the second of her husband's wives and, though she never had any children, Grandmother Aama is considered the heart mother of the children and is caretaker and healer of the household, in effect the mother of the whole family.

Grandmother Aama's home is in Boudhnath, just outside the fabled city of Katmandu. Katmandu, with its many carved rose-brick temples filled with pilgrims, is not a clean city, and it is teeming with monkeys, beggars, and diesel fumes. Like Katmandu, Nepal is a country of spectacular contrasts. Though it is a poor country, it is rich in cultural history and, being located on the highest reaches of the Himalayas, has some of the most stunning scenery in the world. However, the government is unstable from long-standing tensions between those loyal to the king and those aligned with Maoist rebels. Violence can erupt at any time, which is why it was uncertain whether Aama would be allowed to leave her country to join the Grandmothers Council. At the last minute she was given permission, and her powerful ways of prayer will increase and intensify the prayers of all the Grandmothers.

Today, she is standing along with other Grandmothers to spread her message of universal peace, harmony, and brotherhood.

"I am doing my prayers around the world to create a world without war and tension," Grandmother Aama says. "I want to see this world full with natural beauty, where everybody will have equal rights and opportunity to share nature's womb."

Julieta Casimiro

Mazatec

(HUAUTLA DE JIMENEZ, MEXICO)

GRANDMOTHER Julieta Casimiro is a Mazatec elder. She lives in the Sierra Madre in the state of Oaxaca, Mexico. She is a mother of ten, a social support in her community, and she is a curandera, a healer. For the last forty years, people from all over the world have come to her to partake in her ceremonies, receiving much healing and life guidance.

Grandmother Julieta was seventeen years old when her mother-in-law, herself a healer in the Mazatec tradition of sacred plants, introduced her to the "holy children," Teonanacatl, the sacred mushrooms. Grandmother Julieta took the mushrooms many times with her husband's mother and deepened her relationship to God with the wisdom gained. With all the knowledge she acquired, Grandmother Julieta was inspired to invite people to journey with her and to share her work with others. Teonanacatl literally means "Flesh of the Gods" and is the basis of an important and sophisticated spiritual tradition in Mesoamerica, dating back as far as 5000 B.C.E.

"Because we don't have money for doctors, we heal ourselves with the mushrooms," Grandmother Julieta explains. "It is believed that God gave the mushrooms to the peasants and those who could not read in order for them to be able to have a direct experience of Him. One does not have to be afraid of taking them. These sacred mushrooms give you light. They give you the light of understanding, of knowledge, and the light of truth, wisdom, and wonder."

For Grandmother Julieta, the Lady of the Moon, the Lady of the Sun, the Lady of the Stars, and always the Virgin of Guadalupe are present in her work. The Virgin of Guadalupe is the protector of all beings in Mexico. She is the human physical embodiment of the ancient earth goddess Coatlique, who was revered by the pre-Hispanic civilizations for thousands of years. Guadalupe's apparition in 1531 took place at Tepeyac, a hill outside Mexico City, which was Coatlique's place of worship.

This sacred feminine presence is in the center of Mexico's religious life today and is an anchor to all healing practices involving the use of sacred plants. The powerful relationship Grandmother Julieta feels with Guadalupe fuels her: her life and the space of her work with essential feminine qualities such as compassion, patience, grace, and eternal love are all grounded in earthly symbols and in invisible energies.

"I do my work because the Virgin of Guadalupe illuminates it and gives the light of knowledge," Grandmother Julieta says. "She is really close to me. I feel Her, and She gives me the strength to pray and sing."

When Grandmother Julieta works with people, she always starts with prayers. She begins her work by lighting thirteen candles. In the ancient Aztec tradition, thirteen was the number of realms one had to go through before reaching the divine layer of consciousness. The creation of the context for the ceremony is an important part of her work and is approached with a great deal of reverence. The use of copal as incense, candles, honey, cocoa beans, and the saying of the rosary all constitute specific elements of preparation for the guide and for the participants. They create a container for the night's work and forge alliances with the Spirit World, spirit helpers, and spirit supports.

"It pleases the angels and it pleases the saints when I work, to make offerings to them that way," she says.

The ingestion of the sacred mushroom is approached with a great deal of respect and a lot of faith. The mushroom is chewed with the front teeth only, as it is not considered food in the Mazatec tradition. The number of mushrooms is intuitively decided by Grandmother Julieta, as she gets to know the participants prior to the ceremony. The experience of relinquishing ordinary states of consciousness can be intimidating for some people at first. Grandmother Julieta decides how to introduce people to the journey space with gradual intakes. When the participants are familiar with the journey space, she takes people into deeper regions of their inner world with larger amounts.

Ingesting the sacred mushrooms and being guided by a curandera, one dissolves the surface layer of consciousness, exploring one's layers of fears, opening to profound visions, and gaining mystical knowledge, Grandmother Julieta explains. The merging into a state of spiritual illumination expands into the transpersonal and into an experience of enlightenment.

"For the work to go well, I am always invoking God," she says. "This way the people feel well and are also able to express what they are experiencing. Each head is its own world. One works gently, very sweetly, until the effect of the mushroom is gone."

The night's work can last from six to seven hours. When the work is complete, Grandmother Julieta closes the work with a prayer and gives thanks to the Divine for bringing its light into the people's lives through their journey.

"The people are happy with the wisdom they gather," she says. "They gather this wisdom and elevate themselves to the Lord to reach the light of understanding."

The sacred mushrooms are the "medicine" in Mazatec culture. For physical ailments, emotional imbalance, family tensions, and focusing intentions through prayers, the mushrooms are revered as powerful guides and "doctors." By shining the light of understanding on one's source of inner tension or illness, they open the passage for healing to take place and, by doing so, rebalance the entire system on physical, emotional, spiritual, and energetic levels.

"During the session, the patient is able to feel where the illness is in their body," Grandmother Julieta explains. "Then light is evoked to cure the illness."

Grandmother Julieta works with people with AIDS, cancer, emotional disease, immune deficiency, stomach and digestive problems, skin conditions, and varied psychosomatic symptoms of inner imbalance. Because the patient and the healer are working with energy and Spirit, the mushrooms can heal many illnesses in one overall imbalanced system, as opposed to the need of specific pills for each disease in the Western medicine system. However, if the patient is severely ill or has been ill for a long time, Grandmother Julieta refers them to a Western doctor.

"Some people are not able to feel the effects of the mushroom and are not able to open their hearts or their minds to enter the world of the journey," Grandmother Julieta explains. "Working with tobacco (called San Pedro by the Mazatecs) can sometimes help those people."

As in many traditions using sacred plants, tobacco is very revered and considered a powerful ally in the work with the sacred mushrooms.

Ingesting the sacred mushrooms and being guided by a curandera, one dissolves the surface layer of consciousness, exploring one's layers of fears, opening to profound visions, and gaining mystical knowledge.

In this tradition, the tobacco is used fresh, ground with lime and garlic, while prayers are incorporated into the ritual of grinding the leaves on a stone. Once prepared, the paste can then be applied onto the patient's body. Its effects are very noticeable and create a quickening of the physical metabolism, a wave of heat in the system, a deeper experience of embodiment. The application of San Pedro is an important part of the ceremony. Invoking the energy of Jesus, San Pedro is applied to the part of the body where the illness is located.

"The blocked energy begins to move from that part of the body and moves down the legs and out through the feet," Grandmother Julieta explains. "No matter the illness, this is how the people are cured."

For some patients the ceremony is a place of expansion and a relaxed state of receiving. For the ones who want to work on their emotional or energetic tightness, Grandmother Julieta works hard with them. Sometimes whole families come to be cured in a ceremony; if envy or anger creates too much disturbance, the whole family will partake in a night's work. Each member of the family will reach personal understanding, will make amends, and all members will create healing rituals shared and offered during the night, until the family's harmony is restored.

"The mushrooms open people's hearts, and they need not be afraid," she says. "When my patients leave, they feel very satisfied, happy, feeling good. When they thank me, I say, 'Thank God.'"

Addressing the Grandmothers Council for the first time, Grandmother Julieta blessed herself and offered a cup of water to the four

directions. Expressing what an honor it is for her to be there, Grandmother Julieta said, "All of us here want the same thing. We want to walk
in peace, and we want no more war. We don't need war. All the suffering
and pain that is going on in the world, especially of little children and
elders, really hurts me inside. Our Mother Earth is hurting. They are destroying our Mother Earth. They are destroying our Mother. They need
to have respect for Her. We need to walk with respect, especially during
these times we are living in now. I pray hard all the time for this to
change. I carry my rosary with me everywhere. It is an honor to be here
and to pray with all the Grandmothers. I hope you like my words."

Julieta
Casimiro

Other Women Elders

THE WOMEN of the Hudson River Indian tribes, hosts of the Grand-mothers in New York, spoke of a legend handed down that tells of how peace was kept among the tribes because the grandmothers of the clans often visited each other, to ensure goodwill among all the people. And then the men had to follow their example. In that same spirit, the Grand-mothers met with women elders representing many different walks of life. Together, they sought to find new solutions to the mounting prob-lems of our troubled world.

The Grandmothers would say that, at the Spirit level, the selection of women elders was not random or accidental. At the same time, as with the Grandmothers, many other wise women of the world would equally qualify.

Alice Walker

For one of the world's most esteemed writers, Alice Walker—author of the Pulitzer Prize–winning novel *The Color Purple*—it was the emotional legacy of her family's ancestral stories that caused her to seek out in-digenous ways of healing.

The youngest of eight children, Alice was born and raised in the small farming community of Putnam County, Georgia. Her parents were sharecroppers, and sometimes earned as little as three hundred dollars a year. Her mother was also a domestic and dairy woman. The family lived in shacks, hovels where the landlord would not have kept animals. They were at the mercy of the weather—the extreme heat and cold of the

South. But through her own vibrancy, Alice's mother was always able to remind her children that life on this green planet is paradise.

"I was not permitted in a sense to become completely cynical or feel abandoned or depressed for very long," Alice says. "I could see through my mother that we were living in magic, that this world is all magic. My mother showed me how in nature we are never alone. She could grow anything. It was like living with a goddess."

Recently, while walking through a field filled with wildflowers, a friend commented to Alice about how much more incredible the scene would look if they were stoned. For Alice, the scene could not have been more beautiful. That is the teaching she received from her mother, that everything is already vivid and powerful.

"I didn't need any enhancement. Nothing needed to be in Technicolor, magnified, no special effects. None of that. That is part of what I have in my spirit," she says. "I'm just so grateful to my mother for that wisdom."

Alice overcame many difficulties growing up, including losing sight in her right eye after being accidentally shot with a BB gun by her brother. But the stories of two of her ancestors, that as a child were hard to understand and as an adult held even greater fascination, were more difficult to resolve. One story was of a Cherokee ancestor, Alice's connection to native peoples, who was violent and mean from being horribly abused. The second story that haunted Alice was about her father's mother, who was murdered for her great beauty in the churchyard by a man whose desire for her could not be controlled. She died in Alice's father's lap and was blamed for her own murder because of her beauty. Alice's grandfather became an alcoholic as a result and abused his next wife.

"I have been working with family stories, with this sense of deep wounding."

"I have been working with these family stories a lot," Alice says. "This sense of the deep wounding we have. How can we remember that the people who came into our families 150 years ago were not merely the little sliver of information that was passed down, like 'She was so beautiful; she shouldn't have been so beautiful'?"

In the past few years, Alice has explored her family stories using the plant medicine Ayahuasca, a medicine that the indigenous peoples of the South American Amazon have used for many thousands of years.

"Ayahuasca and medicines like it deal with the need to realign with your own soul and your own soul in relation to other souls, who were wounded and basically remained wounded," Alice explains. The term *medicine* in indigenous cultures applies to anything that heals body, mind, or spirit.

From her experiences with Ayahuasca, Alice came away with the strong conviction that it is essential to protect natural medicines. "The way pharmaceutical companies are going, the way society is going," Alice believes, "it is almost impossible to treat our illnesses, our deep soul wounds. We can pacify them. We can make ourselves be cheerful zombies with pills, but we can't heal because the drugs are silver bullets aimed at a small portion of the problem, not at the whole thing. Traditional medicine is always administered in the context of ceremony, which gives it a different complexity, and so the healing happens in the body but also in the psyche."

Alice believes traditional medicines have taken hard hits from the church and the dominant society, which has never understood and called heresy the fact that people who use them are freer and have their own independent connection to the Divine. Alice has personally been approached by eight different shamans seeking her help in keeping their traditional medicines from being declared illegal and from being patented by Western pharmaceutical companies. Traditional medicine requires more than just popping a pill. The result is her latest novel, *Now Is the Time to Open Your Heart,* written in part to try to keep Ayahuasca from being patented, which is what she says the pharmaceutical companies want to do.

When introducing herself to the Grandmothers, Alice revealed, "I come from the South, but before coming from the South I think I must have come from the stars. I feel so entirely at home both on Earth and in space."

Gloria Steinem

"I come from the tribe that has lost its memory," admits the eminent feminist activist and writer, Gloria Steinem. "And the loss of memory is the root of oppression."

For Gloria, it was significant to be with the Grandmothers Council on the land where "the idea of the possibility of the suffragette movement was fostered"—and in the part of the country that was the heart of the Underground Railroad. "I truly appreciate that in a profound way we are overthrowing everything here," she commented to the Grandmothers. "We are trying to learn again."

Gloria is a legendary figure in the women's movement in the United States, but her insights, passion, and drive to advocate for women were born out of personal hardship. It wasn't until she was well into her fight for women's rights that Gloria became fully conscious of what motivated her.

Ruth Steinem, Gloria's mother, was an intelligent, college-educated woman who suffered from severe bouts of depression and spent most of her time in bed. Her psychological illness produced hallucinations and at times violent and self-destructive behavior. The family traveled the country in a dome-covered trailer nine months out of the year so that her father could buy and sell antiques from California to Florida. Only the summers were somewhat carefree, when her father returned to Ohio to operate a small resort. When she was able to, Gloria's mother tutored Gloria and her sister, instilling in Gloria a deep respect for books and a love of reading. For the most part, reading was Gloria's only escape and pleasure.

"The loss of memory is the root of oppression."

The family split up when Gloria was ten, and her mother became very ill and unable to take care of herself. That job fell to Gloria and, in effect, she became her mother's mother, taking on the complete running of the household. They lived in a worn-down house with no heat and had to sleep together in the same bed to keep warm. The lower part of the house was rented out to meet basic expenses, and Gloria earned extra money as a tap dancer. Gloria excelled in school, and in 1952 she entered Smith College.

While at Smith, Gloria began to understand some of the factors that contributed to her mother's depression. Before she was married, Ruth Steinem had been a successful column editor for a newspaper in Toledo, Ohio. But when she got married, she felt she was forced to give up her career to fulfill her roles as wife and mother. Having both a career and a

family was not socially sanctioned. The devastating impact of such restriction was a catalyst in Gloria's drive to change society's views of
women. Adding fuel was her realization that her mother's condition
was never taken seriously by the medical community, precisely because
she was a woman.

At the same time that she was gaining insight into her mother's
plight, Gloria also discovered that her own grandmother had been a
suffragette, helping women to earn the right to vote. Her grandmother's
example inspired and emboldened Gloria to fight for her convictions.
She emerged from Smith an activist.

Over the years, Gloria experienced the pain of inequality firsthand
in her career as a journalist, and she grew to connect with the oppression of all women, no matter their color or race. Today she is interested
in exploring the cultures of indigenous peoples, the origins of gender-
and race-based caste systems, how gender roles and child abuse lie at the
roots of violence, the methods of nonviolent conflict resolution, and
how to organize across boundaries for peace and justice.

Her definition of feminism is "the belief that women are full human
beings." She sees that the women's movement was in a way about becoming each other's mothers. "In a deep way," she says, "so many of us
had mothers who were unable to be powerful in the world."

In the end, Gloria believes we are not here to save other women, but
in a profound way to save ourselves. "I have faith that, if we do the hard
work of learning what has gone before us," she says, "taking on the pain
of others, as well as their pleasures, of honoring the self-authority of
each person, including ourselves, then these days will have made us a
multitude."

Carol Moseley Braun

"I represent the newest people on this planet," says Carol Moseley
Braun, the first African American woman to be elected to the United
States Senate and to run for president. "Disconnected from their roots
and culture when they were brought to America as slaves, African
Americans have had to recreate themselves," she explains.

Today, it is difficult for most black Americans to know from which tribe or part of the African continent they originated. In addition, once the Africans arrived in America, their families were torn apart, for many over multiple generations, so that their once-deep roots can seem very shallow. Slavery, it was once noted, is America's original sin.

At the bedrock of the founding of America is the forced separation of both Africans and Native Americans from their land by people who intentionally left theirs. Because the Native Americans still live in their original part of the world, they still have remnants of their culture and access to their ancestors, whereas African Americans have been completely cut off.

"The result for black Americans is that we have come together in this country to create a new people," Carol says. "As a result of the genocide of both Africans and Native Americans and the native people's kindness and goodness to the Africans, the two peoples have intermarried. Because the native people were so welcoming, most black Americans can draw on the Native American blood in their families for some sense of roots."

In the context of world societies, Africans see black Americans as American, while most white Americans see blacks as African. "What I do is wrap my arms around myself and say I am all of those things: I am African, American, new, and indigenous," Carol says.

Carol believes that slavery and the treatment of blacks called forth a strength in the people. Blacks feel the pain and trauma of the violence of the past, and of the evil that gave rise to all those horrendous situations, and they have a choice. "You can get busy living, or you can get busy dying," Carol feels. "It's a choice each one of us has to make ourselves. As an old gospel tune says, 'You've got to serve somebody. It might be the devil or the Lord, but you've got to serve somebody.' To me that means you serve by either your actions or your inaction, by what you do as well as what you fail to do. We can choose to create community that will help heal the world, help all to survive and thrive, or we can let evil continue to rampage around the planet."

Carol was born in Chicago. Her mother was a medical technician and her father worked in law enforcement. He was also a musician, mastering seven instruments, and he spoke several languages. Her great-grandmother was a midwife who concocted her own medications, salves, and potions, so Carol grew up with a strong belief in traditional healing methods. From her parents, Carol learned the necessity of hard work and the importance of education. She received her law degree from the University of Chicago, while working at the post office and at a grocery store.

"I have had a difficult life, a life filled with a lot of pain," Carol says. "For me, the challenge has always been in finding resilience and in searching for light, reaching for joy and staying one step ahead of whatever would make me captive of that pain. That is why the Maori teachings about time have meant so much to me."

In 1992, Carol was elected to the United States Senate and, in 1999, President Clinton appointed her as ambassador to New Zealand. In her two years as ambassador, Carol, who was made an honorary Maori, learned a great deal about indigenous ways and experienced true spiritual healing.

The Maori have a unique view of time. Where linear-thinking Westerners see time as a continuum, the past as something behind us, over and done with, and the future as that which is ahead of us, what we look forward to and move toward, the Maori view the future as what is behind us and the past as what is ahead.

"The future is unseen, so it is actually behind us, unknown and unknowable," explains Carol. "The importance about this change in perspective is what it says about the present. In the Maori view, the future is created by actions in the present. The future is the legacy of actions taken today. And so, in this view, if you keep your eye forward on the lessons of the past in the present, the present is strengthened and helps you create a better future, a future that is better than the past you inherited."

From the Maori perspective of time, Carol learned to look at the past in terms of qualities gained: perseverance, the ability to build community and create hope in people that tomorrow will be better than yesterday was. The Maori teachings offer the opportunity every day to commit to life and create a different future.

"In this context," Carol explains, "I look at the absolute necessity of facing the past, being honest about what it is, not pretending that past events didn't happen, or don't really matter and have no relevance today. Unless you look honestly at the past, you can't draw on the strength that has brought us this far, that strength that will help us create a more joyful, enlightened, and loving future. The legacy of strength developed from the past will create a better future, one that builds on pain without giving in to it."

"Disconnected from their roots and culture when they were brought to America as slaves, African Americans have had to recreate themselves."

Carol believes the Grandmothers Council is a service to create community, to bring people together, and to magnify the good. "We can be a force to resist and fight evil," she says. "And to engage in this world today to make certain that the anger, injury, and violence of the past do not become our legacy to the next generation, that we do make a better future."

Tenzin Palmo

In a small cave, isolated by the formidable mountains and unrelenting snow and cold of the Himalayas, Tenzin Palmo spent twelve years alone in intense Buddhist meditation. By herself, she faced wild animals, survived avalanches, and came close to dying from starvation. She grew her own food and slept upright in a traditional three-foot-square meditation box.

Entering her cave with a vow to achieve enlightenment in a female body, no matter how many lifetimes it took, Tenzin ended her twelve-year retreat fully dedicated to helping promote the spiritual guidance of women.

Born Diane Perry, the daughter of a fishmonger in London's East End, the woman who was to become a Buddhist legend grew up as an ordinary teenager with a boyfriend, a job, and a big crush on Elvis Presley. At eighteen, she read her first book on the little-known subject of Tibetan Buddhism and, discovering a strong identification with the teachings, bought a one-way ticket to India when she turned twenty.

In India, Tenzin joined a Buddhist monastery to become a nun in the Drukpa Kagyu line and found herself the only woman among hundreds of men. She quickly came to realize that males dominated the spiritual traditions of Tibet. In fact, women were considered unclean because they menstruated and were banned from participating in many of the rituals, ceremonies, and traditions. They were also barred access to certain holy places.

Knowing such restrictions were contrary to the Buddha's true teachings, which stressed the importance of women in society and their equal right and ability to gain spiritual liberation, Tenzin took it upon herself to break down the widely held belief that had evolved through a patriarchal system, that only men could attain enlightenment.

When she entered her cave, no one believed Tenzin, being a woman, would last in such harsh conditions. Because no woman had gone before her and men had little interaction with women and even less knowledge of the issues specific to women for such an undertaking, Tenzin was entering uncharted territory when she entered her cave and was literally forging a new path for women.

"I had planned to stay in my cave forever," Tenzin said. "But life has a way of serving you up with what you need, rather than what you want."

Before his passing in 1980, her guru, His Eminence the Eighth Khamtrul Rinpoche, made several requests of Tenzin to start a nunnery. In 1992, the lamas of his Khampagar Monastery at Tashi Jong again made this request of her, and finally Tenzin felt ready to take on the challenging process of raising funds and establishing a Buddhist nunnery in northern India. One of the aims of the Dongyu Gatsal Ling Nunnery she founded is to revive the tradition of female yogis called "togdenma," which means "realized one." Not one of the yogis of this tradition is known to have survived the Chinese takeover of Tibet. Their training is the same rigorous, long, and austere process that Tenzin followed.

Tenzin's life is now wholly dedicated to promoting women's self-discovery, self-appraisal, and spiritual enlightenment, and to giving women the guidance for their journey that she never received. Her acclaimed book, *Reflections on a Mountain Lake*, is a great resource for Westerners, both men and women, trying to understand and apply the Buddhist teachings. She plans to establish an international retreat center where Buddhist laywomen and nuns can spend time in retreat in a safe environment conducive to spiritual contemplation and growth.

Living in a cave taught Tenzin how to be independent and self-sufficient, and how to deal with her thoughts and problems by herself. Above all, she came to know herself. As reluctant as she has been to be part of the world again, Tenzin sees how being involved in society develops the higher qualities of being human, such as compassion, generosity, and patience.

"I had planned to stay in my cave forever, but life has a way of serving you up with what you need, rather than what you want."

"It is our true nature that we are trying to realize," Tenzin believes.

In that vein, Tenzin feels it is time for the male religious leaders to stop overlooking half the human race and include women's voices in their dialogues and decisions. They would serve themselves well, she believes, if they would learn to develop the feminine side of themselves that is already an innate part of their own nature.

Helena Norberg-Hodge

A leading analyst of the impact of the global economy on local cultures, Helena Norberg-Hodge was born in New York City and spent most of her childhood just outside the city of Stockholm, Sweden. She attended universities in Austria and Germany, where she studied philosophy, psychology, and art history. Afterward, Helena traveled to Italy, France, and Mexico, and by age twenty-five spoke six languages fluently. In the early 1970s, she worked as a linguist in London and Paris.

In 1975 Helena was asked to be part of a German film team going to a remote part of the world she had never heard of called Ladakh, also known as "Little Tibet," located in the trans-Himalayan region of Kashmir. Though in the western part of Tibet, Ladakh belongs politically to India. As a linguist, Helena was asked to go along in order to try to pick up some of the complex language, to facilitate the making of an anthropological documentary.

Helena was not thrilled at the prospect. After her extensive travels, she wanted to finally put down roots in Paris. But she consented, thinking she would be in Ladakh for only six weeks. As it turned out, the trip completely changed her life, and Helena considers the work this initial trip inspired over the next thirty years to be both a great privilege and a great burden.

Before leaving for Ladakh, Helena felt she knew most of what was happening in the world. She had a broad international experience of many cultures. "Most people had never heard of the place in 1975, and many still haven't heard of it," Helena says.

What Helena discovered in Ladakh were the happiest people she had ever seen. No one had been allowed into the country since the 1940s, and before that its remoteness protected the culture from being changed by the colonialism and Western imperialism that had altered so many other indigenous cultures.

The people Helena encountered in Ladakh had a remarkably high standard of living, despite living in the harsh conditions of a desert twelve thousand feet above sea level, with only glacial mountain water for irrigation and a four-month growing period. Their art, jewelry, and architecture were beautiful, and life moved at a gentle pace unimaginable in the West. A young guide named Dawa, when asked to show Helena the poor section of a remote village on her first trip, was puzzled by her question. He told her there were no poor people in Ladakh.

"That first trip to Ladakh, I saw with my own eyes that it is possible for people, when they are free, to create wealth out of a barren desert," Helena says. "I saw that it is possible to live differently, to live in a way that is truly more sustainable and that is truly more peaceful and joyous and happy, when people are free to develop according to their own values and their own needs."

In 1977, after her work in Ladakh with the film crew, Helena studied linguistics at Massachusetts Institute of Technology with Noam Chomsky. The next year, she returned to Ladakh with the English barrister John Page, a man she had fallen in love with and would later marry. By then, the Indian government had thrown open the doors, and external forces began to cause massive and rapid disruption in Ladakh. A once-proud and self-sufficient people were being demoralized and debilitated by contact with the modern world.

In a chance meeting, after years of no contact, Helena met her first tour guide, Dawa, again. "Dawa had become a walking advertisement for Western fashion," Helena says. "Metallic sunglasses, a T-shirt emblazoned with an American rock group, skintight jeans, and basketball shoes. I told him I hardly recognized him."

Helena believes that the global economy and those running the engine are "imposing a structural violence on the world," whether consciously or unconsciously. "The messages of the Grandmothers, the message from indigenous cultures and peoples around the world has been managed, marginalized, brainwashed, and corporatized in a way," Helena explains, "that has made it very, very difficult to get the message out."

Since observing that poverty around the world is the product of an expansionist, global, colonial economy, Helena has fought to rebuild the strength of local culture and economy and to apply what she observed in Ladakh to battle the effects of the global economy worldwide.

For the past twenty-five years, Helena and her husband have lived six months out of the year in Ladakh. Her inspirational book *Ancient Futures: Learning from Ladakh* has been translated into forty-two languages and made into a film. Helena has dedicated her life to getting the message out about the importance of localized economies. She has founded the International Society for Ecology and Culture, is on the editorial board of the *Ecologist* magazine, is a cofounder of the International Forum on Globalization and the Global Eco-Village Network, and is a recipient of the Alternative Nobel Prize.

> *"The messages of the Grandmothers, the message from indigenous cultures and peoples around the world has been managed, marginalized, and corporatized."*

Luisah Teish

Author and priestess of Oshun, the goddess of love and of the waters in the Yoruba Lucumi tradition of West Africa, the Caribbean, and South America, Luisah Teish grew up in the segregated South in New Orleans, Louisiana, the daughter of parents who presented her with an eclectic assortment of religious traditions.

"During the slave holocaust," Luisah explains, "Africans brought to America were not permitted to practice their traditions under penalty of death. We had to be Christian in order to be a proper slave. However, we quickly learned that the practices of the Native Americans were very similar to our own and, along with an overlay of French, Spanish, and Portuguese Catholicism, merged our practices with the native people. We also adjusted by identifying our African deities with Catholic saints."

Her father's side of the family was African Methodist Episcopal. They were second-generation servants, one generation away from slavery, on an Irish plantation. Her mother, who was a combination of black Haitian, French, and Choctaw Indian, was trying to be Catholic.

"So I grew up with my mother making moccasins, picking herbs, and performing rituals, and my father telling her to stop doing 'that stuff,'" Luisah says. "Since he was no longer on the plantation, he was trying to prove he was a civilized man."

Luisah believes it takes years to unravel ancestry. When she was little, she wondered why her mother and her friends sat around and interpreted each other's dreams. How was it that her mother could go out in the backyard, make a circle of salt, do some chants and ritual, and bring down rain? Why didn't the women in her neighborhood act like the women on television?

"But, thank goodness they didn't!" Luisah says.

As a little girl, Luisah watched the women in her neighborhood closely. They were a community of herbalists, midwives, trance mediums, and storytellers.

"From them I learned that a woman's ability to produce and nurture life gave them special powers—an ability to interact with natural forces in ways uncommon to men," she says. "They depended on each other to divine the meaning of dreams, to foresee and prepare for natural disasters, to heal illness and deliver babies, and to perform rites associated with physical growth, spiritual development, and death. These women were well-informed community organizers who settled family disputes, raised their hands against injustice, and could be dangerously inconsolable when offended. I have learned that women like these exist in every culture on the globe."

Following the request of her father, Luisah's mother raised Luisah Catholic. But she couldn't go to the local church because it was segregated. She had to go to the church two towns away, which meant she had to stand on the highway to catch the colored people's bus, which was dangerous because she could get shot at by a Klan member.

"I had to learn to run away from the Klan in between waiting for the bus," she says. "I came up at a time when black folks had separate water fountains and had to go to the back door to go up the stairs.

"Being Louisiana Catholic is not like being any other Catholic. It is more Caribbean Earth-based than anything," Luisah explains. "So I grew up taking holy water from the church, bringing it home, putting it in a bucket with brown sugar and the morning's first urine, and mopping the floor with it to keep the evil spirits out of the house. A picture of Saint Michael hung over the front door overseeing everything."

An open and sensitive child, Luisah had frequent visions and was intrigued by all the magic going on around her. With both sides of the family pushing their different religious agendas, her mother simply told her, "God by any means necessary. Go to any church you can, learn whatever you can, and do that."

But once Luisah discovered the "old folks" everyone was always talking about were Africans and understood that Africa was her mother-land, everything opened up for her. The first time she experienced Spirit as spoken of in her African culture, she was in college and performing the sacred dances of the Pan-African tradition. She began to feel an energy running through her body and knew then that Spirit was not just an abstract concept. Her eclectic search for spiritual insights led her to conclude that each tradition contained both truth and fallacy. In time the elders of the Oshun tradition told her she was born to be a priestess, not a dancer.

As a little girl, Luisah watched the women in her neighborhood closely. They were a community of herbalists, midwives, trance mediums, and storytellers.

Luisah was put through eight years of purification before she was initiated as a priestess of love, art, and sensuality. For twenty years, she has been a "Mother of the Spirits," and then after four more years initiated as "Mother of Destiny." She was given guidelines for the rest of her life, according to the contract she made with Creation when she incarnated on Earth.

"I was told it was my job to tell the stories that further kinship between the people of the Earth," she says. "Stories that inspire respect for the forces of nature and help us remember the goodness of the ancestors, with an emphasis on the work of women."

Today, Luisah teaches classes on African goddesses, shamanism, and the Yoruba Tambola tradition. She is author of *Jambalaya: The Natural Woman's Book of Personal Charms and Practical Rituals, Carnival of the Spirit,* and *Jump Up.* She is founder of Ile Orunmila Oshun (the House of Destiny and Love), the School of Ancient Mysteries/Sacred Arts Center, and the director of Ase Theater. She has performed her dances of world mythology and feminist folklore in Europe, South America, and New Zealand.

Wilma Mankiller

The first woman to be elected principal chief of the Cherokee Nation, Wilma Mankiller gave a keynote address at the Grandmothers Conference and was an important part of the dialogue on many issues.

Wilma grew up dirt poor on the land of her father's ancestors just outside Tahlequah, Oklahoma. For supper, the family often ate squirrel and other small game. Their home had no electricity, and coal oil was used for illumination.

The Cherokee Nation occupied the Carolinas and Tennessee until their forced evacuation to Oklahoma by the United States Army, which came to be known as the Trail of Tears. Along the way to Oklahoma, thousands of men, women, and children died. For over a hundred years afterward, the Cherokee were considered wards of the state, until in 1970 the United States government allowed the tribe to elect its leaders directly.

Two decades before autonomy was restored, Wilma's father moved the family to the Hunters Point district of San Francisco, hoping to provide a better life for his wife and children. Wilma was eleven. The move was part of the Bureau of Indian Affairs relocation program originally developed for Japanese Americans during World War ll. A social engineering experiment, the program uprooted Native Americans from rural areas and found them jobs in industrial cities. Whether intentional or not, the program weakened ties to the reservations and diffused any political clout the native peoples might have had.

Wilma lacked sophistication and had a difficult adjustment to city life. Eventually, the city's diverse population introduced her to many cultures. Her father continued to instill pride in their heritage, which was fostered at San Francisco's Indian Center. But Wilma had no interest in academics, no plans to go to college, and no real aspirations. After a whirlwind courtship, she married a middle-class Ecuadoran college student and had two children.

They shared a comfortable life until Wilma's activism was awakened in 1969 when a group of university students occupied Alcatraz Island in order to gain attention for the issues impacting their tribes. Not long after, she began working in preschool and adult education programs of California's Pit River tribe. Her activism was creating a huge chasm of understanding with her husband, and after eleven years of marriage they were divorced. Wilma returned to her ancestral home in Oklahoma, where she immediately became an advocate for her people of the Cherokee Nation, helping them get grants and launching important programs.

The resiliency of Wilma's people is the direct result of their culture, which has been sustained since time immemorial.

Wilma enrolled at nearby University of Arkansas. One night, while returning home from class, she was involved in a head-on collision. The driver of the other car, one of her best friends, was killed, and Wilma barely escaped with her own life. It took seventeen operations to save her right leg from being amputated. Her long recovery proved to be a time of deep spiritual awakening.

Then in 1980, just one year after the accident, Wilma was diagnosed with myasthenia gravis, a disease that causes weakness in the voluntary muscles. Dealing with a chronic illness made her understand at a deeper level just how precious life is. Soon after, she developed the Bell Project, which taught communities how to revitalize themselves instead of waiting for help from outside sources. As a result of the Bell Project, Wilma became nationally known as an expert in community development.

Wilma married a longtime friend and a former director of tribal development, Charlie Soap. Triumphing over yet another physical disability, when she received a kidney from her brother in a transplant operation, Wilma decided to run for chief of the Cherokee Nation. She believed she would be better able to bring to fruition the many community projects she had initiated. Wilma's candidacy in 1987 met with violent opposition. Her car tires were slashed, and she received many death threats throughout her campaign. But Wilma prevailed, and her historic election resulted in a great deal of public attention for the Cherokee Nation, which revitalized the entire tribe. Wilma believes the resiliency of her people is the direct result of their culture, which has been sustained since time immemorial.

For Wilma, spirituality is the key to both her public and private life. Her understanding of the interconnectedness of all things, an ancient teaching of her tribe, is what sustains her and creates her passion for developing healthy, viable, independent communities. This understanding has made her a significant spiritual force in the United States.

Her Holiness Sai Maa Lakshmi Devi

Considered a blessed Indian saint and revered spiritual teacher, H. H. Sai Maa was born of Indian parents on the African island of Mauritius. Growing up, she suffered a great deal of pain from observing but not understanding the injustices of the world. How could some people live in small huts in poverty when others lived lavishly in big, beautiful houses? Traveling to Europe, she saw beggars and disabled people whom no one seemed to care for. It was like a knife piercing her heart. Her parents were worried about her extreme sensitivity, and the teachers at school complained that she didn't play with other children.

This world was not offering the love H. H. Sai Maa felt from the beautiful beings of light that had been visiting her since she was four. These beings she trusted more than any human, and she considered them to be her true friends. She came to learn that the beings were ascended masters, in India called *siddhas*. There it is believed that because matter is merely a form of light, some humans are able to perfect and transmute the gross matter of their physical bodies into light to become beings of light. Jesus is believed to be one such ascended master.

"I was uncomfortable on this planet until I was fourteen," H. H. Sai Maa explains. "There was something in me that was pulling me somewhere else, and it was painful. I even wanted to kill myself."

From memories of previous incarnations and from a deep inner feeling she could trust, she knew that within her she contained the knowledge of a better way of living. Her inner world had always transcended time and space. The normal world made her feel contracted. But it was the unbearable contrast between her inner and outer worlds that was bringing her to her spiritual awakening. She began to feel comfortable on this planet when she became a disciple of Sai Baba of Puttaparthi, India, in her early teens. He has been her only teacher.

"There is a perfection in all of us that we must tap into, a consciousness of beauty, abundance, purity, and harmony."

A more profound understanding of love came to H. H. Sai Maa in her early twenties, when she was in Europe, alone for the first time and missing her parents terribly. Her intense sobbing took her to another state of consciousness, where she saw something grander, something greater and deeper. Her relationship with God became stronger, and she found herself hoping to find a way to uplift humanity, to learn how we can be better human beings.

"There is a perfection in all of us that we must tap into," H. H. Sai Maa believes. "A consciousness of beauty, abundance, purity, and harmony."

H. H. Sai Maa feels it is not a requirement to be part of a particular religion or even a part of any religion to have a spiritual awakening. What is important is moving away from worshipping things of the material world and moving toward finding the Divine within ourselves. In fact, one of H. H. Sai Maa's strengths is her ability to transcend and work with religious leaders and people of many traditions around the world. Growing up, she had attended Muslim, black African, and Catholic celebrations. On the small peaceful island of Mauritius, families of several different religions lived together on the same courtyard with no problems. Though most were immigrants, everyone was united. All spoke Creole and danced on the beach together.

As with many masters before her, H. H. Sai Maa believes that there are only two energies that we are dealing with, and they are love and fear. Fear is the root cause of anger, jealousy, and disharmony, whereas peace and harmony come from love. Our hearts are either contracting from fear or expanding from love. "There is nothing else," she says. "Everything is in between or a mixture of the two."

For H. H. Sai Maa today, being in the human form is the most fabulous way to experience God fully. "Life is so full of juice. It is so sacred and so powerful. We cannot keep missing it."

Today, H. H. Sai Maa has many disciples from around the world and is involved in many humanitarian projects worldwide. Addressing the Grandmothers, she said, "The grace of Divine Love of the Great Mother has brought us together again. Let us cherish each other with great respect."

H. H. Sai Maa was awarded a very rare and significant title, 1008 Mahamandelshwar, which means "Master of Many Ashrams." She is one of the few women ever to receive this title, and the only non-India-born woman to receive it in the title's thousands-of-years-old history. She is the author of *Petals of Grace: Essential Teachings for Self-Mastery,* and her organization is called Humanity in Unity.

PART TWO

Guidance for Our Times

Prophecies

THE GRANDMOTHER OF ALL CREATION, the One who is the maker of life, the One whom we have forgotten, is calling us. She is not angry with us, but She is sad that we have forgotten who She is.

She is coming back into our consciousness through prophecy and visions. She is bringing a profound nurturing, a depth of compassion, and a kind of love we no longer remember, but which was strong in ancient times. This pure female energy will awaken in men as well as women, through a story we will already know in our hearts once we hear it.

The return of the Grandmother has been foretold for hundreds of years. A vision of the Grandmothers Council has been seen by many peoples, indigenous and nonindigenous alike. The Grandmothers are gathering because, according to the prophecies of many religious traditions, the end of the world as we know it is near. The Grandmothers tell us that balance as a way of living is returning, balance in all relations, including with our Mother Earth. A thousand years of peace is being ushered in for those who will make the necessary changes in their hearts.

The Grandmothers say that the circle of life was broken around five hundred years ago when the white people first came to the Americas. They came, according to Hopi legend, forgetting the original teachings of the Creator. When He gathered the peoples of the Earth together on an island that is now beneath the waters, He told them, "I am going to send you in the four directions, and over time, I am going to change you into four colors. But I am going to give each of you certain teachings, and when you come back together, you will share these teachings with each other. Then you can live together and have peace upon the Earth, and a great civilization will come about."

The teachings foretold that when such a time came, it would be the people of the white race, the guardians of the fire element, who would begin to move upon the Earth and reunite us as a family. But many of the people of the fire forgot the teachings about the sacredness of all things, and their violence against the native peoples, the land, and so much of nature destroyed the Earth's balance and dissipated the feminine energy of the planet. Many tribes became extinct, and much of the wisdom held by the indigenous Grandmothers was destroyed with their passing. If they weren't murdered, the Native Americans starved to death when they were put on land that nobody else wanted. This cruelty toward indigenous peoples, lands, and traditions has spread throughout the world. Now there are many countries where women and children are being treated inhumanely and where the Earth is being destroyed. The Grandmothers believe that Mother Earth Herself is saying this all must end.

It was at the time of the holocaust of the native peoples of the Americas when the prophecy about the return of the Grandmothers was revealed to a few, and then the story grew so that the people could have hope and prepare. Because of the prophecy of the Grandmothers' coming, many native peoples are finding it in their hearts to forgive the unspeakable atrocities that their ancestors and the creatures of their land have endured. Sadly, however, many still cannot.

As the Grandmothers tell it, prophecy is a message from the Spirit World and is most often given in response to a deeply held prayer, one that may not even be conscious. Receiving a vision or prophecy is a mystical experience of seeing or knowing. Prophecy can unfold into consciousness as a story originating in the heart. When a prophecy is given and begins to unfold, it is because a greater intelligence is guiding its unfolding. As the prayer is clarifying itself, the keepers of the prophecy, the people who have open dialogue with Creation itself, never reveal the whole story at once. As with a puzzle, different pieces of the prophecy are revealed and confirmed in different ways and in bits and pieces to different people, sometimes over a long period of time. If we are holding a piece of prophecy, we may not know it for many, many years, until the right time comes. Prophecy manifests in this way so that all isn't lost if the one or few people who hold the whole story pass away.

The Grandmothers say that receiving prophecy isn't like opening a door and having all meaning flood out at once. Once prophecy is set in motion, it is ever evolving. As the story is forming, its meaning is not always clear. But, just like a powerful and affecting dream, a prophecy reveals more and more levels of itself as time passes. A vision or prophecy feels more real than waking reality and teaches truths too deep to be adequately conveyed in words. When a vision or a prophecy is received, its power and strength and future unfoldment won't let you go, won't leave you alone until it's fulfilled.

Grandmother Bernadette explains, "Each one of us receives prophecy from where we are." The visions we receive speak to just who we are in time and space as individuals, as nations, and as the children of Mother Earth. With the prophecy will come a new level of awareness about why we are placed where we are when the prophecy first reveals itself to us. In the same way that pieces of a prophecy bring people together, parts of one's own life can take on new meaning when a prophecy is revealed. Earlier events in our lives suddenly seem connected to the prophecy. We come to feel as if a seed had already been planted in preparation.

Throughout the ages, human survival has depended on prophecy. Certain members of a tribe—shamans and medicine people, those with a greater gift for accessing and traveling in the other realms of consciousness—trained their bodies and their minds to become finely tuned receivers of this knowledge and guidance. Native Americans have traditionally gone on vision quests, which involve days of isolation, fasting, and prayer in pursuit of guidance from the Spirit realms of existence. However, the spiritual realms are accessible to people of any cultural background. We can connect with our spiritual vision during times of deep intuition, through powerful dreams and in expanded states of consciousness, such as during meditation, self-hypnosis, or while taking sacred plant medicines.

The Grandmothers teach us that time is not linear in the Spirit World. All time exists at once, enabling the seeing of events far into the future. Some of the greatest prophets and seers of the world's religions have been able to see hundreds, if not thousands of years ahead. However, prophecy is ever evolving in response to the positive or negative direction that human society may take. Dire prophecies are fulfilled when humanity refuses to change.

As an example of how prophecy unfolds over time, Yupik Grandmother Rita Pitka Blumenstein tells the story of a wooden bowl that her grandfather made her when she was a little girl. All the other bowls he made for family members were decorated with ravens, loons, or other birds and animals. But Rita's was decorated with a spiderweb in the center and a spider in the corner. Distressed that her bowl was not like the others, Rita asked her grandfather why she had a spider when everyone else's bowl was decorated with beautiful animals.

"He laughed, scratched his head, and told me, 'That's a future communication,'" Rita explained. "When I first heard about Web sites, I said to myself, 'There's my bowl'!" (The spider is the communicator in her tradition.)

Though the Grandmothers Council had been seen in many visions and been foretold for hundreds of years, it was Jyoti's vision of a sacred basket that set the prophecy in motion. At the time of her vision, Jyoti was not aware of the prophecy about a Grandmothers Council.

As the Grandmothers each took their seat for the first time at the circular council table, the prophecy of their coming together continued to reveal itself through each of their stories. "Today, yesterday, thirty years ago, we are standing in the movement and vibration of the sacred prophecy about the Grandmothers Council," Mayan Grandmother Flordemayo told them.

With regard to their role in the prophecy, the Grandmothers believe they are hundreds of years late, that this council should have been formed long ago. All of the Grandmothers brought a sense of urgency to the table, as they met privately in council for the first three days. "This is the eleventh hour," said Hopi Grandmother Mona Polacca.

A Critical Crossroads in Human History

On Hopi land, there is a sacred boulder called Prophecy Rock, which displays a time line of coming events. At one point, the time line splits. One branch of the line stands for the one-hearted people. At the end of that line is a drawing of a man holding a staff and a flower, representing life and happiness. The other branch of the line represents the path of the two-hearted people, the path of the people who live only by the laws of materialism and technology. The figures on that branch are depicted with their heads separated from their bodies. That branch dwindles, breaks off into chaos, and finally fades away. Just after these two lines split, there is a line that connects the two lines one more time. That line represents the short time we have left to choose the path we will follow.

Some of the most ancient prophecies about present times are from the Mayan culture, which names the year 2012 as being the end of the world as we know it. Yet, at this pivotal point in time, the Mayans say we still have choices. The Mayan calendar is based on cycles that represent the movement of the Earth within the heavens. According to Mayan prophecy, during this short period of time we are entering a photon belt—a region of space radiating intense electromagnetic energy that our solar system encounters every twenty-five thousand years, and that always ushers in a new age.

"Time is of the essence," believes Mayan Grandmother Flordemayo. "During this time, it is essential that we move as quickly as light into the Light. Otherwise, the higher and higher spiritual vibrations within this short cycle could leave many behind. To think that in a hundred years, we've lost total consciousness of everything. We humans have disrespected so much that in this time of movement, where the celestial doors have opened and heavenly beings are coming from the four directions to help us, if we don't do what we've been asked to do, well . . . the results will be sad. We must learn how to wake up and stay awake during these dark and changing times."

The Hopi also call our times the Purification Times, and prophecies speak about the cleansing of the Earth. Some of the worldwide environmental changes that have been foretold in native prophecy already have come to pass: the greenhouse effect, changes in the seasons and in the weather, famine, disease, the disappearance of wildlife, and the hole in the ozone layer referred to as "the hole in our lodging." Native peoples are especially upset about flights into space. The Hopis saw the space station hundreds of years before it came to pass, and now say that it is upsetting the Earth's balance more than anything else. Already space is being polluted by our debris, just like the waters and the air have been. The space station is seen by many indigenous tribes as signaling the beginning of the end.

When Grandmother Clara of the Amazon was visited by the Star Beings, they also confirmed that the timing of the event that will herald what they called the "Galactic Dawn"—a mass awakening of humanity to our cosmic origins and intergalactic relationships—is to be in the year 2012.

"What I see today in the world," says Grandmother Clara, "is a lot of darkness and a few points of light trying to illuminate us as we go through the dark tunnel of our Age. We Grandmothers here are holding each other's hands, illuminating this path, so that we can bring health to this Mother Earth and heal the wounds She is suffering from, wounds made by ignorant men, ignorant of the truth of the Light and of the Creator. The message from the Beings of the Stars is that it is necessary for everyone to open their hearts to the truth of the Spirit, of the Spirit World, as it is this truth that will lead us to our salvation."

Throughout the ages, human survival has depended on prophecy.

Humanity and the Earth are being cleansed of the accumulated negativity caused by humanity's greater orientation to the material world and to technology, which has caused us to lose our connection to the Spirit World and to nature. We are destroying our planet and ourselves as a result of our materialism. Since nature is the source of our visions and centers us in Truth, the more we destroy nature, the less able we are to live in balance and wisdom and the more wars, disease, and disharmony we create.

The Grandmothers say that the Earth's changes will bring about an awakening of spiritual consciousness of the people. Only when the ego is dropped can the voice of Spirit be heard. Most often it is in times of crisis, when our egos are humbled, that we are able to receive intuitive impressions and spiritual knowledge. Humanity can always be counted on to respond to huge natural disasters with aid and prayers for those affected, and, for a little while at least, to reunite the world.

As Grandmother Agnes says, "The Spirit World is just a breath away, right here for us to tap into. We Grandmothers of the council are being nudged by the Grandmothers and Grandfathers of the Spirit World that speak through us from there. Without Their power and great strength, the Grandmothers Council would not have been formed. As carriers of our traditions handed down to us since time out of mind, I believe the Creator has a script for us, and we just have to act it out. He nudges us when we need to act or speak or stop and just listen."

All the Grandmothers believe we must develop a different relationship with Creation itself, or else humanity will continue in a fragmented and dangerous direction, and there will then be no hope for turning our troubles around. Though the prophecies that speak of great changes to Earth are dire, the Grandmothers believe that the times will only affect those who do not heed the warnings. They say people will need physical, mental, emotional, and spiritual strength to change themselves; otherwise a huge portion of the population will suffer immeasurably. Sadly, because the majority of humanity is not spiritually but instead materially oriented, it is feared that many people's reaction to the immense stress of the times, which they might not be able to handle emotionally, will be to destroy everything around them.

During her prayer with the Grandmothers in New Mexico, Nepalese Grandmother Aama Bombo called out the names of the gods and goddesses from her home country and environs. She called upon Kali, the female goddess who can take the form of the Destroyer, to help the Grandmothers show the way.

Aama conveyed Kali's thoughts: "Kali is not happy with what is going on in the world," Aama said. "She sees that humanity is lacking in good values, and she is not happy with the cruelty of the people, who have been killing each other every day just to fulfill their selfish egos. They are poisoning the Motherland and the sky. This has led to the suffocation of all the creatures, who are not allowed a fresh breath," she says. "Spirituality and its values have been subordinated to the ego and to injustice."

The prophecy of the Grandmothers says we must learn again to love one another. The people who will survive are those who love and affirm life in every way. But we must be willing to make conscious changes in the way we view life and in our actions toward all of Creation. The survivors will be people who are open to a whole new level of consciousness and seek true communication with the Earth and the Creator.

From the experience of her own transformation, Grandmother Clara feels the key to changing is to learn to believe in oneself. "I was so ashamed of my powers. Everyone has an inner gift and a mission, even though they might not know they have it. We all have the capacity to do many things, especially if we open our hearts. Mother Earth can help us. We should give more and more value to ourselves, not allow negativity to take hold of us in our daily lives. That is what is happening on this planet. Dark spirits are ready to go to those negative places. In these changing times, we must cling to God, to the great spirit of Truth, to the light that radiates its crystal-clear rays. We must work with the sacred knowledge that exists on our planet."

Grandmother Flordemayo says the Mayans are among those whose prophecy reveals that a new consciousness is preparing humanity for the spirit of the feminine, and the spirit of the Grandmothers, when humanity will walk from the four directions into the light at the center. To the Mayans, the jaguar represents the spirit of the feminine. She carries on her back the universe and is fearless, swift, gentle, fierce, smart, and beautiful.

"I come from the Star People of the Pleiades, and I am also a child of Central America," Flordemayo explains. "In our oral teachings, we were told that at this particular time it will be the women who lead the nations. I bow to the spirit of the women from the beginning of time, the spirit of woman that is within all of us. Male/female, female/male—we all come from that One. We are also told that at this time it is the energy of the stars that will move the nations."

Grandmother Maria Alice of the Amazon has been collecting confirmations of prophecies she's heard from her elders since she was a child. "We, too, have the prophecy that says that it will be the women who will lead this last time of transmutation," she says. "And here we are."

After Sebastião, a leader of Maria Alice and Clara's spiritual community, passed into Spirit, another one of their spiritual leaders, an older man, began a strict fast during what he knew would be the last year of his life. He didn't eat or drink anything except the holy medicine, Santo Daime.

"As a result," Maria Alice says, "he was constantly listening to the divine songs. During that time, he received many messages from Spirit for the women. He was told that women would transmutate first, then men, that women had never to doubt this task and take it in their hands. He saw that men should take over women's work and give them space to do whatever they wanted, because the women would be showing a different way of being in this world. Nature is showing the signs, and already women are changing."

Nature Is Our Guide

The Grandmothers say that nature is prophecy, that wisdom is embedded in the very threads of Creation. The spiritual power of the Earth and the heavens releases dormant wisdom and creates moments of transpersonal guidance. At this time, the Grandmothers say, we are being nourished with a new, purer energy transmitted by nature and the universe, which will help us meet these challenging times with integrity and grace.

For Grandmother Mona, prophecy is not something that is somewhere in the distant future, but is continually being expressed through nature. "I was always told to look around me," she says. "Look at the water, the wind and the air, the fire, even the sun. Nature is telling us what we need to know. We must have concern for the prophecies for the sake and love of our people and for the generations to come."

While growing up, Lakota sisters and elders Grandmothers Rita and Beatrice Long Visitor Holy Dance were told by their grandmother that the ancient prophecies were already being lived out. Nonnative people were coming to their land, and the sisters were told to take care, even when they walked and fished. They remember airplanes dropping bombs onto the Badlands, just as had been foretold. They witnessed the machinery that had been seen in visions begin to damage the sacred Black Hills area and destroy the holy places of the Lakota people. The sisters' greatest concerns are the Lakota land and the sacred Black Hills.

"Our delegates and chiefs haven't been able to do anything about this, except talk," Grandmother Rita says. "I bring this sad news so that I can maybe take back hope to my people. Somehow, the nonnatives have to understand the importance of the Black Hills to us. We want to give something good to the unborn who are yet coming, the future generations."

The Lakota know that their language and the land are one. If they lose one or the other, they are no longer who they say they are.

"Prophecies are living words that we have to be about in our everyday lives," Grandmother Beatrice explains. "Our grandmother always advised us to keep about ourselves, keep our thoughts together, keep our work going on. And pray, so that when you go through the difficult times, you have a lightness about it."

The Lakota people have a special relationship with the elements, and the elements have told them that Grandfather Rock is the first Grandfather. The rocks were here first before all the rest of the world and hold all memory.

"The world was created around Grandfather Rock," Grandmother Beatrice explains. "So it is a living prophecy, living words we honor every day through prayer. A prophecy can change. We can tell the spirit of Grandfather Rock that we can't handle something, and He will take it on, because He will know what to do with it, how to go about it when we don't."

For Grandmother Mona, prophecy is about concern and love for people and the generations to come. Her grandfather, the last chief of the Havasupai Indians, told her the legend of a particular rock on their people's traditional lands, where in ancient times, a turtle would come and speak to them telepathically.

"The turtle would tell the people about how to live, what kind of season to expect and how to prepare, how to behave toward one another, and how to stay strong as a nation," Mona says. "He taught the people how to keep their guardian spirits in good favor by how they lived. In those early times, the turtle spoke of many things to come."

THE CONDOR AND THE EAGLE

One of the most important prophecies the Grandmothers share about this time in history is the prophecy of the Condor and the Eagle. Though there are several versions, there are essential elements in all: According to

ancient legends, the North and South American continents were one
land long ago. Then a great shaking took place, tearing the continents
apart, leaving the people divided and forcing them to take different
paths. The path of the people of the South American continent, called
the People of the Condor, represented the heart, intuition, and mys-
ticism. The people of the North American continent represented the
brain, the rational mind, and the material worlds. Prophecy stated that
in the late fourteen hundreds, the two paths would converge and the
Eagle would drive the Condor to near extinction. Then, in five hundred
years, a new epoch would be possible, when the Condor and the Eagle
would have the opportunity to reunite and fly together again.

"It is prophesied that the People of the Center, the people of Central
America [which in legend also includes Brazil and other parts of South
America] in the land of Brazil, the Amazonian land, is where all the different cultures will come together for peace," says Grandmother Maria
Alice. "Already many different Indian nations are gathering together
there, sharing rituals and sacred medicine. Japanese, Africans, Europeans, Americans, Chinese, people from all over the world are coming
together to share hope. They are blending traditions without suppress-
ing each culture's truths. The gatherings are teaching forgiveness, to forgive all enemies of the past, all the misunderstandings of the sons of the
Earth. Mother Earth is showing us how, the forest is showing us how."

The Grandmothers know that both peoples need each other. The
People of the Eagle have developed an extraordinary intellect, which
has created the modern, technological world, but at the expense of the
heart. The People of the Condor, the indigenous peoples, have developed a depth of heart-centered wisdom from their intimate relationship with nature, but have become materially impoverished.

The Grandmothers say both the Eagle and the Condor have much to
teach each other. When the Eagle and the Condor once again fly wing
tip to wing tip, it will herald a time of partnership, love, and healing,
and the Earth will come back into balance. When the People of the
Eagle help the Condor soar again, they will cease making the choices
that are destroying the Earth, and their own sense of isolation, unhap-
piness, and stress will vanish. Together, they will make a new design for

the children and for future generations, for the good of all life everywhere, and destiny will be fulfilled.

The bald eagle in North America had nearly become extinct like the condor, but its survival in the United States has been fought for under the Endangered Species Act and today it is no longer considered endangered, though it is still considered threatened. Condors have not been seen in Oregon for over two hundred years, but Grandmother Agnes is thrilled to learn that two condors have recently been born in captivity there. The condor is said to carry the spirit of the ancient Thunderbird, a legendary raptor that existed in ancient times when the first people lived on the North American continent. Larger than both the eagle and the condor, the Thunderbird was said to be gifted with the great power of sight and was able to transmit telepathically ancient wisdom and knowledge in prehistoric times.

"It is going to be a wonderful thing, when the Thunderbirds come home," says Grandmother Agnes. "We hope the Eagle can carry our message to the Sky People and the Creator and help us with our prophecies. I do believe we will see a change, as the prophecies state. Our prayers are for the whole world, for all the people. We are at the threshold. But it is up to the women. We are the ones who can carry more than one spirit in us. We are what I call 'multi-modal': we can carry a child, stir a stew, and kick the cat out all at the same time!"

"With every new experience, we have the power to redefine ourselves, so that no matter what our past mistakes, we can always change."

For Cheyenne Grandmother Margaret Behan, the word *resilience* is especially significant and important when understanding the role women will play in fulfilling the prophecies. "There is a saying among my people, that our nations shall continue until the women's hearts are on the ground," she says.

THE BUTTERFLY

Grandmother Mona believes the Hopi legend of the butterfly can see us through these turbulent times of darkness and confusion by revealing to us our path of transformation. These times can actually then be viewed as necessary to enable humanity as a whole to transform into a comprehension of the truth of our oneness with each other and with all of Creation. Only by going into darkness and breaking down our old ways can we move from the myopic view of the caterpillar to the greatly expanded view of the butterfly—a necessary view if we are to save the beauty and resources of our planet for the next seven generations to come. Then we will have emerged out of the darkness of ignorance into the beauty of the butterfly to see the wonder, hope, compassion, faith, and charity so essential for our survival.

Yupik Grandmother Rita Blumenstein explains that with every new experience, we have the power to redefine ourselves, so that no matter what our past mistakes, we can always change.

"The past is not a burden," Rita says. "It is a scaffold which has brought us to this day. With this understanding, we are free to be who we are. We create our lives out of our past and out of the present. The quicker way to heal is by going forward, however—not by spending a great amount of time and energy dwelling on the past. We are our ancestors when we heal ourselves. We also heal our ancestors, our grandmothers, our grandfathers, and our children. When we heal ourselves, we also heal our Mother Earth, and we heal future generations."

The Power of Prayer

Grandmother Julieta of Mexico is able to see prophecy by being in continuous prayer. "I live in that place of the power of prayer," she says. "What I see is that unity is what the world must strive for now. In this unity form, everything comes together again. All our relations come together again in circles of people, who are at peace again within themselves and also patient with the ones who have not arrived at such peace yet. These circles need to be formed everywhere, so that we can become one again on the whole planet, in this visible world and in the invisible world."

To Grandmother Julieta, the prophecies are just tests given to us by the Creator so that we can and will move forward with faith. "We need to study, though we think as adults we know so much," she says, "because everything that is happening is happening for a reason."

Grandmother Flordemayo believes that it is only by living in the moment, moment by moment, that we will save ourselves, because when we are living in the moment we feel more alive, more love and community. "If we pray 100 percent in that moment, we can move the consciousness of humanity," she says. "The period of scattered prayers and scattered wishes has ended. We must pray to the spirit of the heavens and the Earth, the spirit of the sacred waters, the spirit of our Mother Earth. We must pray to the spirit of humanity to acknowledge each other as brother and sister, as nations of people that breathe the same air, as nations of people who are being fed by the spirit of the ancestors of the sacred waters. If we do not acknowledge this, we will lose our way. So I pray for the moment. I pray to be totally present without ego, with total passion, with total love to Spirit, because it is the only way."

When the attacks of 9/11 happened, Flordemayo says she did not know which way to turn to pray. But then she went into intense prayer and asked the Grandmothers from the Spirit World to give her even a little understanding. "That was my prayer day and night, day and night," she says. "On the seventh day at the seventh hour, exactly the same hour things happened in New York City, the north wall in my bedroom seemed to disappear. As I opened my eyes, angels began to appear in a circle. They were so big they might have been ten to eighteen feet tall. They had huge wings that touched the sky and the earth. In the middle of the circle was a holy man. The angels began singing a mantric sound. The sound was so celestial, I don't have words to express it. The sound of their singing emanated throughout the universe. They sang towards the One, the perfection of Love, Harmony, and Beauty, the only being united with all the illuminated souls who form the embodiment of the Master, the spirit of guidance, a Sufi prayer by Sufi Master Hazrat Inayat Khan. I still cry when I see and feel them."

Flordemayo believes that all who are conscious of peace and prayer are in that sacred circle of angels, a part of that glorious vibration in sound and song. "This is who we are," she says. "I pray we can carry this

beyond the Earth to the universe. It is not just about the Earth anymore.
It's beyond and into the universe."

The Prophecy of the Grandmothers Council
Continues to Unfold

During their private council, the Grandmothers decided they would
visit one of each of their homelands every six months. In New Mexico,
they were visiting the current home of Flordemayo. This time, they were
hosted by the Tewa Women United.

During one of their first nights there, Grandmother Bernadette had a
vision of a place where the Grandmothers were to gather, a place that would
be known for their work and would become a place of pilgrimage. She saw
that each of them would lay a large stone solidly in the ground, and that the
thirteen stones would somehow be connected to each other in a big circle.
That night, Yupik Grandmother Rita and her traveling companion, Marie,
both saw a vision of an enormous whale.

The next day, when Bernadette told Jyoti about the vision, Jyoti told
her that only the day before she had learned about a man named James
Jereb, living forty minutes away in Galisteo, New Mexico, who had a temple dedicated to the spirits of the ancient Grandmothers and Grandfathers. For the temple, thirteen huge stones had been erected in a circle,
each one embedded three to four feet into the earth. On hearing of Bernadette's vision and learning there was already such a place nearby, the
Grandmothers decided to contact James Jereb about visiting his temple.

Eight years before, James's life had radically changed, when he entered a large medicine wheel in Sedona, Arizona, just to be polite to his
friends, who were believers. To his shock, when he reached the center of
the medicine wheel, he was met by the spirit of a Blue Star Kachina, a
man who appeared to be a giant with long flowing hair. The work of
a Blue Star Kachina is to serve as a bridge between the fourth and the
fifth worlds. An archeologist and art historian, James considered himself to be left-brain oriented and didn't believe in the validity of visions.

The Kachina told James that the man he thought himself to be was false, and from then on, James would discover his true self. After this extraordinary awakening, James began accessing various masters from the higher realms of consciousness. Afraid and confused at first, he nevertheless followed instructions they gave him for his new life and new work.

Although James had never painted before, he became a visionary artist and learned that his own spirit was that of a temple builder. Over time, he created Stardreaming and built eleven stone temples and a fairy ring on his property in Galisteo. The temples were all dedicated to cosmic principles. When the temples were completed, Lilith, whom James considers his "main goddess," came to him and said, "Behind all the gods and goddesses are the Grandmothers and Grandfathers. We all have Grandmothers and Grandfathers, even the Divine Mother. You must build your last temple to them to fulfill prophecy and help usher in a new world."

"We must learn how to wake up and stay awake during these dark and changing times."

James was given a vision of a circle of thirteen great stones surrounding a huge spiral of illuminating light created by white crystal, which he called the Temple of Magic. He brought the stones from a hundred miles away on a flatbed truck. The largest stone weighed eighteen tons. Each stone, James says, was chosen under the guidance of the Ancient Ones, whose temple this was. It was to be a sacred site for the Rainbow race. He was told that, by opening our heart to the stars, we can experience the magic of oneness. James and those helping him discovered that each of the stones had its own character. Work on the Temple of Magic was complete on the winter solstice of 2004, a day of unusually heavy snow.

Two days after Bernadette's vision, the Grandmothers visited the Temple of Magic. They had asked if they could perform a ceremony there to consecrate the temple. James agreed.

When the Grandmothers entered the land of Stardreaming, Rita and Marie spotted the whale of their visions, a huge one-hundred-foot whale made of stone.

As the Grandmothers approached the temple, each intuitively chose her stone. Without realizing it, Grandmother Agnes, the oldest member of the council, chose the oldest stone. Grandmother Rita from Alaska, who was wearing a necklace adorned with bears, chose the bear stone. Mayan Grandmother Flordemayo chose the stone with Mayan glyphs. All the Grandmothers were amazed that there was a perfect stone for each of them.

Grandmother Bernadette was to lead the ritual. The Grandmothers sat in chairs in front of their individual stones, as a beautiful full moon hung low over the gathering. None of the stars were visible yet. No one, including the Grandmothers, knew what to expect.

A fire was lit in each of four fire pits, each pit carefully placed at the midpoint between the four directions to symbolize moving into a new world. Bernadette began her ritual by ceremonially "waking up" the spirit of each of the stones. Her sacred staff was powerfully charged. Each of the stones elicited a different song, different prayers. As the ritual proceeded, the night sky became filled with millions of stars, and it seemed like the very heavens touched the earth where the Temple of Magic and the Grandmothers stood.

To everyone's amazement, when the ceremony was over, the Grandmothers said all the gods and goddesses had passed through with their blessings, and that we are now in a new and sacred time.

Since the Grandmothers' ceremony, many magical changes have come about for people visiting the temple—especially women who have come seeking answers and have then had miracles occur in their lives. The temple is now imbued with a tremendous sense of reverence and an unsurpassed feeling of awe and unconditional love.

For too long have this wisdom and the ancient prophecies been forgotten, and like leaves falling to the earth unheard and unseen, the ancient teachings have been trampled on as if nothing of importance lay beneath our feet, teachings so near and yet so far from our thoughts and memories. It is the hope and prayer of the Grandmothers here and in Spirit that this profound feeling of unconditional love will ignite the consciousness of all peoples around the globe, and we may all finally share the oneness of our hearts and minds as foretold in the time before time.

Women's Wisdom

"TODAY'S CIVILIZATION has been cut loose from the essential roots that formed humanity," says Grandmother Bernadette.

Those roots, the Grandmothers say, reach deep into the Sacred Universe, the domain of Spirit where feminine and masculine energies are in perfect balance and harmony, and where the unity and connectedness inherent in all sentient beings is revealed. However, in today's world the power of the feminine—the most potent, loving, and creative of forces on Earth—is severely suppressed, and if not again honored the imbalance of male and female energies could cause the destruction of humanity, if not the Earth Herself. This female power that sustains the Earth and all Her inhabitants, and that is so essential for the survival of the planet, resides within each one of us, man and woman alike.

Because the male energies of the world are now in control, power is not balanced with unconditional love, and aggression, greed, and fear dominate humanity. Women, children, and all of nature are being exploited, with devastation the result. Even the provenances that have been in the safe and loving hands of women for thousands of years have been usurped. Since the beginning of time, women have successfully governed their bodies and the cycles of conception, pregnancy, and birth, only now to be dominated by those with their own agendas of power and control. This is not the way of the Divine Feminine.

WOMEN CARRY the ancient knowledge of the Divine Feminine deep within the very cells of their being, the Grandmothers say. Because their bodies are subject to the great cycles of the moon and stars, women's wisdom is connected to the very heavens. Their natural wisdom about the rhythms of birth, life, and death are far greater than a man's can be, and should never be subject to any religious or judicial law.

Remember, the Grandmothers say, we women have been gifted—we are all-knowing, the creators and makers of life, the seed carriers of the children of the Earth. We must be strong and walk in our innate knowledge and power under the protection of the four directions. With the world on the brink of destruction, women must wake up this great force they possess and bring the world back to peace and harmony. When women and men set in motion this enormously transformative feminine force of unconditional love they carry within, great healing and change will come about.

Depending on our spiritual or religious devotion or our culture, the Divine Feminine may come to us as Shakti, with the electrifying vitality that ignites the flame of life. She may come to us as the Virgin of Guadalupe or the Blessed Mother Mary, whose gentle hearts have an infinite capacity for enduring grief and sorrow, as She comforts the most humble, modest, and often-forgotten of our brothers and sisters. She may manifest as the radiant light being, Tara, Mother of the Victorious Ones whose infinite wisdom fills an infinite sphere. Or Quan Yin, the bodhisattva of infinite compassion. She may speak to us as the Black Madonna, the embodiment of all that is sacred on this Earth. She may come to us as White Buffalo Calf Woman, who brought to the Lakota people their sacred pipe, with which they walk like a living prayer, a bridge between the sacred beneath and the sacred above. She may enter our bodies through communion with Her plants as She heals, nourishes, and transforms us. Her manifestations are not confined by any specific people, place, belief, or time. We meet Her in meditation, prayer, and visions, in the person sitting next to us, in our mothers and fathers, in the children we love, and within ourselves. And others meet Her through us.

Grandmother Bernadette reconnects with the spirit of the feminine in the forest. "In the forest, I still know how to become one with a landscape rich with a thousand mysteries," she says. "The forest permits me to capture the secrets of the invisible, of which we are the trustees. These secrets will soon become precious compasses for humanity."

Grandmother Bernadette says the Divine Feminine as expressed through nature teaches us to accept the Other and honor and cherish our differences. Next to the grandeur of our Mother Earth, we can see the "fragility and infinite smallness of humanity, the vanity of our excesses, and the ephemeral nature of existence." The force of peace and united families is more deeply understood. And we learn a respect for humanity and nature, now so cruelly lacking in this world.

Tenzin Palmo explains that feminine energy takes whatever form helps people to tap into it. "It's not like the different goddesses are all in their own special heavens with the door closed," she says. "All are archetypical manifestations of this universal female energy. Access is not an energy outside ourselves, but an energy within. Outside/inside, in ultimate reality, it makes no difference," she explains.

Tenzin points out that it sometimes helps to observe the feminine energy outwardly in order to absorb it within. Traditionally in the Tibetan religion, after having received an initiation of a deity, one sees oneself as the deity. It is very important to realize that it is not to something "out there" that we are supplicating.

"It is our true nature that we are trying to realize," Tenzin says. "In the Tibetan Buddhist tradition, you go about the day seeing yourself as Tara and recognizing Tara in others. And, though you think you are pretending to be Tara, in reality you are Tara pretending to be Mary Smith. And that is the point."

One of the attendees at the conference told the story of discovering "the face she had before she was born," the face of her own Divine Feminine. One night in a Chicago hotel room, she was raped and beaten nearly to death. When she was able to get herself to a mirror to assess the damage, she was unrecognizable to herself. Peering through eyes that were now only pinpoints, she stared and stared into the mirror searching for herself. Finally, after many long moments, she was able to look beyond the horror, the pain, and the trauma, deeper and deeper inside herself, and there she found joy.

"In that moment, Shakti was born," she said. "A flame of energy burst all the way up through my entire body."

As the police pounded on the door, she found herself saying, "Oh wow, this is who I am. I am that!"

The police found her in a state of bliss. Now she says her process is to stay with that core and live from that core. After her experience, she sees how women are genocide survivors from five thousand years of being separated from their innate source of wisdom.

Women should not have to have such extreme experiences in order to remember their essential nature and to access their special gifts as women, the Grandmothers say. In ancient times, most indigenous cultures developed initiation rites to honor a young girl's passage into womanhood at the time of puberty, rites that forever connected her with the spirit of the feminine and opened her to her intuitive abilities and her own unique wisdom. Because of women's attunement to nature and the cycles of the heavens, this passage initiated by the first menses was seen by indigenous peoples as profound and to be celebrated. The rites also ensured the survival of the tribe, because the wisdom of the elders about how to be an adult woman, a mother, and a life partner to a man was passed on. A young girl was given pride about her role as a woman and confidence in her distinctive ability to contribute to the whole. The fact that some cultures have carried these rites and initiations to extremes that we find incomprehensible should not keep us from examining what is good and essential about marking this time in a young woman's life in a profound way.

"Women must wake up this great force they possess and bring the world back to peace and harmony."

In Gabon, Grandmother Bernadette says, as soon as a girl is twelve years old, she has to pass through an initiation. The initiation can last from fourteen to twenty-one days, during which time she is taught the rites and the knowledge by the women elders to prepare her for the life of an adult woman. Initiates come to understand the very core of nature: the language of the trees, of the rivers, and of the birds and animals—the essential mysterious language.

"Our culture acknowledges that the gentle power, the gentle strength, the conserver of our beliefs is woman," Bernadette explains. "Therefore, nothing in our country is done without consulting the women. Our wise people, our elders are like libraries. We consult them whenever we have to make big decisions."

In many cultures around the world, a woman was isolated during what was considered her "moon time." This was not because she was considered tainted during her menses, but because she was at her most powerful during that time. Being so profoundly connected to the heavens and the Earth gives a woman far greater access to her own intuition, her inner voice, and the voice of Spirit. What has come to be called the "curse" is really a woman's greatest blessing. But without the understanding of the importance of taking time to be with oneself and reconnect with one's core and with the spiritual guidance of the Divine Feminine, the energies can turn, causing irritability and physical discomfort. Because a woman's power is so great during menses, people around women at this time can feel the energies and, not understanding them, react in a negative way, instead of being supportive.

Living in the intimacy of the tribal system, women bled at the same time, and the time they shared together apart from the rest of their community was considered very sacred. So many women gathering together at the height of their power was a great force for good, not only for themselves and their families, but for the entire community.

Over several millennia, women's power has been undermined—an extraordinary tragedy for all of humanity, the Grandmothers say, because women's wisdom and their access to the feminine energy in all forms, which is so essential to the healing of the planet, are cut off. The result is women giving over their own power over their bodies to technology, such as during childbirth. We have forgotten the ancient understanding that a woman's body is a sacred temple. In fact, as Gloria Steinem pointed out in her keynote address, in ancient times the interior of a church was designed to replicate the reproductive system of a woman's body. The reverent knowledge was not yet lost that it is through women that God brings life into this world.

Of all the different forms feminine energy can take, Tenzin Palmo says the most common is Mother. "The male deities are like the archetypical Father," she explains. "He is the one ready to administer punishments,

137

and the one whom you are trying to please. Mother, on the other hand, is always around, ready to stoop to pick us up, no matter how naughty, distrustful, or uninterested we are."

Luisah Teish has also experienced in her extensive travels that the need in almost every tradition is to honor the Mother manifestation of female divinity—Mary, Isis, Oshun, among others. Luisah had already been awakened to the power of the Great Mother as it was reflected in the extraordinary women of her childhood.

"Ironically, Western culture associates the legacy of women's power with the 'curse of Eve,' and rarely acknowledges its value," Luisah laments.

We must create new nations of empowered women, the Grandmothers say. And we must act now for the sake of the children and for the next seven generations to come.

"We must not for a moment limit ourselves about what we can do," says Grandmother Agnes. "We must give support and encouragement to each other and to whomever we meet on our path."

In the Lakota tradition of Grandmothers Rita and Beatrice Long Visitor Holy Dance, White Buffalo Calf Woman is said to have told the women of the Lakota Nation that it is the work of their hands and the fruit of their bodies that keeps the people alive. "You are from the Mother Earth," she told them. "What you are doing is as great as warriors do."

When Tibet was still an independent country, women were very powerful, Grandmother Tsering explains. "They could hold the spiritual teachings the same way as the men did," she says. "They also acted as warriors, as strong people, too."

Tsering believes that women are naturally powerful, because they are able to hold their power both within and without. They can do whatever they set out to do, so they must never become discouraged or dispirited but should devote themselves to a spiritual path and to prayer.

WE MUST BE WARRIORS with the power of love, the Grandmothers say. The great goal of the Grandmothers is to unite the hearts of the world. We all share the sun and the moon, the planet and the stars, they say. Our blood is altered when we come together as one people, allowing the Divine Feminine within and without to unite us and free us from fear.

The Grandmothers tell us that together as warriors we need to hold the spirit of the land, the spirit of the ancestors, and the spirit of the people who are resisting the yearning in their hearts, which is the Light. Breathe the light of Spirit in, they say. Move with the Divine Feminine. We are always with Spirit. In that moment between breaths, we feel the Divine in a deeper way, and we are connected again to each other and the magical world around us.

"Everything begins with the breath," says Grandmother Julieta. "Women's wisdom is in all of us, but each woman embodies wisdom in her own beautiful way."

H. H. Sai Maa agrees. "The first thing we did when we incarnated was inhale the breath of life," she explains. "Enlightenment is that space, that gap between the inhale and the exhale where we become so aware. Be where you have nothing to do. Relax in that consciousness. In that state, we enter the kingdom of the self. There may be wisdom in books, but this inner silence takes us into deep inner wisdom. When we focus deep within, we allow our inner power to come forth—the great wisdom we carry at our depths and the knowledge of what is our own unique contribution to humanity. Then, being mindful of our breath takes us into the outer world with more awareness."

To enter into our truth, our power, our divine Shakti, H. H. Sai Maa says we need to be in the energy of love. "There is love and there is fear. Those two energies are what we are dealing with," she explains. "When we live in fear, we contract our energies. Love, on the other hand, is freedom."

The Grandmothers agree that personal healing is the essential first step toward healing the world. We need to strive for the peace of mind that has no price before we can realize peace on the planet, they say. Until we discover and explore the unresolved conflicts within ourselves, we cannot recognize the damage to our world that we unconsciously create, and we will have no access to our inner wisdom.

"To value the world is to value ourselves, something women especially need to learn," says Gloria Steinem. "And to value ourselves is also to value the world, something that men especially need to learn." The synapses and cells in our bodies are said to replicate the number of heavenly bodies in the universe, Gloria explains. Which is why our being balanced is so essential to world peace. "As above, so below" is the metaphysical saying.

Women must begin to work with the sacred knowledge that exists on the planet, says Grandmother Clara Shinobu Iura of the Amazon. But first we must learn again to believe in and value ourselves and not allow negativity to take hold of us in our daily lives. "In these outrageous times we live in," she says. "where killing almost seems natural, dark spirits are ready to go to any negative places in order to keep out the light."

Grandmother Clara used to be ashamed of her powers as a woman. She has since learned through her struggles that each woman and man has an inner gift and a mission, even though they may not be aware of what it is. "We all have the capacity to do many things," she says, "especially when we open our hearts."

IN OUR WESTERN CULTURE, we do a great deal to avoid ourselves, the Grandmothers say. We stay so busy and let our lives take over our inner world. Our desires have no end. We keep ourselves in a constant unsatisfied state of wanting something, and, when we get it, wanting something else. Desire, by its very nature, can never be satisfied.

This becomes a problem for the world when the United States consumes so much of the world's resources, just to feed those desires. H. H. Sai Maa believes that desire is constant and Americans especially never feel fed. "In America, there is no depth, no real roots, no history here, which is understandable when, except for the native people, the country is so young," she says. Despite its problems, H. H. Sai Maa believes that it will be the United States that eventually leads the world back to peace. But that will only happen when the United States ends its desire to dominate the world.

"Personal healing is the essential first step toward healing the world."

When we finally come to the point where we are so unsatisfied, she says, everything will begin to fall apart, and we will have no choice as individuals or as a nation but to search within for the source of true happiness. We will learn that without a connection to our divine nature and

140

to the Spirit World that guides us every moment of our lives, whether or not we are aware of its prayers and hopes for us, no relationship, job, house, or material object will fill that emptiness.

Deep within our hearts is where the peace and the healing will start, the Grandmothers say. Surrender to Spirit. Be silent and listen to the guidance of the ancestors; they are there beside you, whether or not you grew up being told about them.

"We always want to stand in our center," explains Luisah Teish. "In our center, we are able to receive blessings from above and below and from every direction. We always want to position ourselves in the center."

"Life is so full of juice, so sacred and so powerful," says H. H. Sai Maa. "We can't just keep missing it by being out of the present moment."

One way to look at our problems, whatever they may be, says Grandmother Bernadette, is to know that we all walk with a cane in life. "Why a cane?" she asks. "Because it is the law of life that each one of us has something in our heart, a problem that hurts the heart, so that we are all the same no matter how else it appears." The cane teaches us that on the other side of pain and suffering is compassion and understanding.

The past lives within us as the present, Gloria Steinem explains. "The deep, deep bruises and hurts from a collective past or a childhood past may make a blow or even a touch very, very painful in the present, may even make us respond to a gentle touch as if it were a blow."

We women should not be afraid of our wounds, the Grandmothers say. Go inside and touch that place where we feel discomfort, where we feel we've been betrayed, where we have had no support. Take our hands and place them under our abdominal area, H. H. Sai Maa suggests, where all our difficult emotions sit, emotions that don't allow us to go further in our lives. Let our hands be a basket for our painful emotions. Inhale into our abdomen and exhale into our hands our lack of trust, our doubts, our sorrows. See the power. Fill our hands with light and bring all that suffering to the Great Mother in our hearts, to the highest part of ourselves, to be healed.

Yet, we also need forgiveness. "To truly love," says H. H. Sai Maa, "it is necessary to drop the past and say, 'I start over, right here and right now, being a new me.'" Most people are living their lives without being truthful with themselves, she says. "All over the world, most people are not well."

"Blessed be our path," Grandmother Rita from Alaska says. "The future is unfolding its new path. Blessed is the promise of new life."

Grandmother Rita Pitka Blumenstein also believes we need to release our past with all our judgments, because that is when we will be ready to embrace the present and receive the gifts of life. When we release our past and everyone who keeps us stuck there, we are open to the full expressive Light. We give ourselves permission to define ourselves, rather than being defined by others or by past events. We can close the door and move on to other ways of being. We are free to become who we are.

"We are not our past, we are not our present," Grandmother Rita Pitka Blumenstein explains. "We are that which we are becoming." We can create our own life out of the past and out of the present, she says. We have the power to reach into the past according to our needs. "It's good for us to remember that we are here to harvest the knowledge and blessings of our life."

Once we tap into our inner wisdom, bringing light to the places inside ourselves that once were dark, we need to bring our inner self into our daily lives, says Tenzin Palmo. We need to consciously inculcate the good qualities while eliminating the bad ones. "Every part of our daily lives—our relationships, our family, work, and our social lives—is our spiritual practice," she says.

Civilization depends on women's wisdom, the Grandmothers say. Severing the roots to the Divine Feminine has cut humanity off from the great human ideas of courage, charity, our love for one another, God's love for us, and commitment to the human community—ideas that are the foundation of a loving family and a great civilization. Without the balance of female wisdom to bring compassion and an enlightened consciousness, the forces of evil that are so self-serving are eroding our higher natures and feeding our worst fears, undermining the great virtues that make us human in the first place. We are forgetting that, as members of the human family, we are all connected, that what happens to one of us happens to all of us.

"Women naturally see the world differently from men," says Wilma Mankiller. "We see it as less segmented, more connected."

As prophecy states, it will be the women with their wisdom who will save the world. Women must begin to forge alliances that will add strength to their individual voices, the Grandmothers say. Women must rediscover and share their wisdom to ensure the health of the entire planet and humanity by tapping into the vast reservoir of energy that runs beneath our common ground and is creating a new wave of women's power. This reservoir of vitalizing energy is centered around a powerful and universal spirituality, based on reverence for our Mother Earth and a shared awareness of the sacredness and interdependence of all life. The creative power of women united is an unmatched force for good.

"It is my hope that the Grandmothers Council will have a mushroom effect throughout the world," says Grandmother Agnes. "That women will start circling up, come together, and bond together, to help one another be better and stand tall with their voices, to say they've had enough of oppression. It is my hope that they will form matriarchal bridges with each other and be a voice again for our Mother Earth and Her children. The women can hear the cries for help. The elders need to teach the young women to take care of their bodies and walk a good path in life to ensure a good future. Help from the Spirit World for this work is always close at hand."

In Gloria Steinem's experience, nothing gets done unless it's done in groups. "We are communal people. We are people who are mirrored by those around us," she says. "There's no more magic than sitting in a group, sharing experiences, and hearing one woman say, 'No kidding, I thought I was the only one.'" Gloria feels that since we are all so unique, when we find we are experiencing similar things, it must be political, it must be about power, and if we can band together, we can change what is wrong.

One day, five years ago, Alice Walker was sitting with a friend talking about how the whole world seemed to be just slipping out from under us. During their conversation, Alice and her friend realized they really needed to have a women's council. So they decided to put out a call to the people who they knew would say yes right away. Eleven women have been meeting since then.

"We meet at the solstices," Alice explains. "The one rule is that there is never an agenda. If you ever really want to understand deeply that to be a woman is to be magic, be in a circle of women meeting regularly without an agenda. Without an agenda, women automatically create 'enough mother,' and everything gets done."

Alice feels that the ability to get everything done without the masculine linear idea that things have to go a certain way is a suppressed reality of women. "Men must have observed women and been unable to figure out how they did it," Alice believes. "You don't have to remember things. You just have to show up with an open heart."

The members of Alice's group bring food, poems, and teachings. They also bring their hopes and fears. One of the members expressed her fear that she was always afraid that she would die alone. At first Alice responded that we all die alone, but then, upon thinking more about it, realized her response was pretty ridiculous. "I promised her that if I am anywhere on the planet when she is dying," Alice says, "I will be there for her. I can see that knowing this and having the strength of the others in the circle, that she is a more confident person. She's not afraid of death now. And I get to be there. It opens a whole other place in myself that is wonderful."

Women united in close circles can awaken the wisdom in each other's hearts.

Women united in close circles can awaken the wisdom in each other's hearts. If in addition we learn to surrender to the ancestors' guidance, we will learn about our mission together. As the bringers of life, the Grandmothers say, we have no choice but to join together and raise our voices for humanity and for our Mother Earth, for the sake of the next seven generations to come.

The Grandmothers say it is time for the women of the world to own their innate wisdom. With the profoundly loving and sustaining power of the sacred feminine in the very marrow of our bones, women can return the world to the Garden of Eden it was meant to be.

Sacred Relations

EVERYTHING IS SACRED, the Grandmothers remind us. And at the seed of everything is relations.

That anyone is really separate from anyone else or anything that is happening in the world is an illusion, they say. This is true for all the kingdoms of nature, as well as for humanity. Every time a tree is felled in the Amazon, a tree in Africa responds.

"It has taken scientists until the twentieth century to prove what we've known since time out of mind," says Grandmother Agnes: "That we are all connected." Grandmother Agnes calls the lack of understanding of the fact that what happens to one of us happens to all of us "spiritual blindness."

We are all naturally part of the great whole of which only certain parts are visible, Grandmother Bernadette explains, so that our reality is not just made up by what can be seen, but actually "dives deep into the Sacred Universe, into the unity and dynamism of the seen and unseen." The Sacred Universe, the world of Spirit, is like the submerged part of an iceberg waiting to be rediscovered. In essence, we are all cosmic beings, she says. We come from the stars.

"The Grandmothers know we have one Spirit, and we know how to use it," says Grandmother Rita of Alaska. "That is why we know that when we come together with one mind we heal."

The Grandmothers tells us that in the beginning, there was only one Creator—one divine intelligence—and so all things created since the beginning of time are suffused with the same sacred essence. Thus, our very existence on Earth implies a profound spiritual connection to the Earth, to all of nature, and to the Spirit World, as everything is a part of the one divine intelligence inherent in all of Creation. An invisible bond exists among all of humanity and to all of our ancestors, a continuous thread running through space and time.

"Mitakuye oyasin" means "all my relations" in the Lakota language of Grandmothers Rita and Beatrice Long Visitor Holy Dance, and is their traditional greeting, whether meeting one person or many. "All my relations" acknowledges that within each person exists the entire universe: all who have ever lived, all who are living now, and all who are yet to be born, as well as all of nature—our Mother Earth, the sun, moon, planets, and all the stars—all of the Sacred Universe since the beginning and until the end of time.

There is an order and a structure to the universe, the Grandmothers say. All things are dependent upon each other. This is why reciprocity and remembering to hold the relations among all people and all things as sacred balances the universe. Any actions that destroy life lead to imbalance, which is what we are facing in today's world.

We must remember again, the Grandmothers say, that the balance within the whole of civilization originates within each individual. At its most primal, Creation results from the merging of male and female energies, the masculine and feminine principles of life, which must be in balance for life to thrive for each of us and for our planet. When our male and female energies are in perfect balance, our life expands and all our relationships are enhanced.

The traditions of the Grandmothers honor the fact that we are all initiated into and connected with our world at the very moment of our birth through the four basic elements of Mother Earth: water, air, fire, and earth. Our primal connection to the four basic elements automatically connects us in a sacred way to the whole of all Creation.

"We live in water in our mother's womb," Hopi Grandmother Mona Polacca explains. "Moments before we come into this world, the water of our mother's womb gushes out, and we follow behind. That is why the Hopi call water our first foundation of life."

It is not a coincidence, the Grandmothers say, that the Earth has the same percentage of water as the human body does. It is also not a coin-

cidence that, as the sacred waters of the planet—Mother Earth's blood—
are becoming dangerously polluted, we are at the same time forgetting
our innate connection to the Sacred Universe, the only understanding
that will save us.

After we follow water into this life, we take into our lungs our first
breath of air, Grandmother Mona says. And so, for the Hopi, air is the
second foundation of life. Our breath connects us with the air and the
winds, without which we would perish. So, as our air becomes more and
more polluted, we are also damaging ourselves emotionally and spiritually as well as physically.

"Fire, the third foundation of life, was met next, when we were
placed in the arms of our mother and father and all who loved and
cared for us," Grandmother Mona explains. "The Hopi say that our
caretakers build up a fire for us that is warm and welcoming, bright and
protecting like a fire."

At some point soon after birth, we were all laid down on our Mother
Earth. First we rolled over, and then we began to crawl on hands and
knees. Finally we stood on the Earth with our own two feet. So the Hopi
say that earth is the fourth foundation of life.

Unfortunately, Grandmother Mona says, few of us remember that
moment when we first stood in balance with the Earth and could feel
Her power and the security that Mother Earth gives us. But as adults we
can observe the sacredness of the moment when we watch a child's pure
delight in its first steps.

As a result of their understanding of our primal connection to the
elements and to all of Creation, the Grandmothers say the first thing we
should do each day upon awakening is to feel gratitude to the Creator
and to Mother Earth for all that has been put in this world for us.

The Creator is the One who is in the water, Grandmother Julieta
says. "He is the One that is in the fire, in the earth. He's the One that is
in the air. He's the One that lives inside us."

If we consciously greet the water as we drink and bathe in it, for instance, we begin to have a relationship with water, the Grandmothers say.
"We know that the Creator can bless us with answers through water,"

Grandmother Mona says. "That element can help us with an understanding. The more we honor and feel gratitude toward water, the greater the assistance we will receive from it for our lives."

Because of our connection to the elements, we also have the capacity to heal the waters, just as the waters can heal us. The Grandmothers say that quantum physics is proving what indigenous peoples have known all along, that prayer can change the pollution in the waters. The Grandmothers pray every day for the waters of the Earth to become purified again. In the same way, a mother can pray for the waters of her womb to embrace her growing infant with love and gratitude, and her child's life will be forever blessed as a result.

The human race and all of nature are really one great family, the Grandmothers remind us. We are all meant to live in peace on this planet. Just as for a single family, the basis for healthy relationships among the family of nations is love and unity, along with a reverence for all of life. However, in these times, the family is being undermined and is disintegrating, and we are becoming prey for the dark forces of fear, a growing plague for all of humanity. Separation, fighting, and segregation within families and among nations are taking over. Everyone is staying isolated, not understanding anyone else's way. As time continues to speed up, we have no time for each other. No one takes the time to get to know each other. Such isolation creates a spiritual separation, and eventually there is only darkness and negativity.

Families must consciously slow down and simplify their lives, the Grandmothers say, in order to become strong again. Time is a gift. We need to learn again how to operate at the pace of the living world: the plants, animals, babies, and old people can teach us to slow down and live and take time to nourish ourselves and our families.

When the "family fire" is not kept burning, our whole social order begins to decay and fall into disorder. The family unit needs to be preserved first, as that is where strength lies during times of change and calamity. Then the strength of each individual family builds up the strength of the whole of the human race. At the same time, the individual human spirit in not annihilated but is nourished by a sense of being connected to the whole of human awareness. So this is where we can all begin to restore our civilization, not with dogma or rules about what families and nations must do, but with a great respect for what can be learned and applied from the great diversity of the human experience.

"We shouldn't abide by rigid rules," Grandmother Flordemayo counsels. "Instead, we need to open our hearts and allow the teachings of the cosmos to enter our lives, by becoming silent and honoring."

"Breaking bread together is the fundamental core of spirituality," says Grandmother Tsering of Tibet. "The primary point is relationship, relationship with our families and with the land. Happiness comes from honoring our interdependence."

In Tibet before the Communist takeover and the intrusion of Western culture, families were very large, and the children were happy and well adjusted. "Women had ten, eleven, sometimes fifteen children," Grandmother Tsering explains. "Yet they were able to take care of all of them without too much effort. These days, they are allowed only two children and, in taking care of these children, they undergo great difficulties."

When she first visited Ladakh before Western culture had seeped in, Helena Norberg-Hodge discovered that every mother had twenty-four-hour-a-day caretakers for every child. "In the early days of Ladakh," she says, "you did not hear babies crying the way we hear babies crying in Ladakh today, and crying more as well in the rest of the world."

One of the cornerstones of the Tibetan spiritual tradition has always been loving-kindness, Grandmother Tsering explains. The problem today, she says, is that we no longer have the pure love that makes a positive, auspicious connection between people and family members. In today's world, the individuals hold themselves to be most important, and a sense of self-importance leads to competition. When parents go out and suffer to gather lots of money, no one benefits, she says, because the money and material things are not what everyone is really seeking.

"We always talked about loving-kindness in our culture," Grandmother Tsering explains. "We took care of each other and shared our love, before the Communist takeover. Grandparents looked after the young children and were the ones to teach the children to have a positive mind and to do no harm. In fact, grandparents and children sought wisdom from each other. Now, when Tibetan families live abroad, parents are

149

left alone when their children get married, and the very young and the very old are most often separated from each other."

"Today we have generations of children whose grandparents are the television set," laments Helena Norberg-Hodge. "In older cultures, there

"The balance within the whole of civilization originates within each individual."

was always an intermingling of all ages with each other, and children grew up with living role models, males and females of all ages. There was a daily connection between the youngest babies and the oldest people. Being toothless, they looked much the same. Fundamental to a rich culture is a connection between the very oldest and the very youngest."

Children need to know about the joys of interdependence and the happiness that living with such a structure brings, Helena says. Spiritual teachings are always reminding us about oneness and interdependence with each other and with the nonhuman world. Interdependence brings the immeasurable gift of being seen, loved, and heard, which allows us to be loving and tolerant in return. This is the way of sacred relations, the Grandmothers say, and the way things are meant to be.

Taking care of children and creating peace ought to be our greatest priorities, Grandmother Tsering believes. "Science isn't really that important," she says. "Nor is the amassing of wealth. The most important thing is to make good people, good human beings. How we teach children affects the world, because eventually they will go on to teach their children what they have been taught. The mothers of our future are being taught right now. What are we teaching them? For the future to go well, we need a very good and auspicious connection. We need the thought of benefiting others to be uppermost in our minds. This is extremely important."

When children are not brought up to have a positive mind, they become a problem for society, says Grandmother Tsering. The responsibility for teaching the children is mostly up to the parents. "Our first teacher is our mother," she reminds us. "She is the one that teaches us right from wrong. When the mother trains her children well, by the time they enter school they will already be good people."

Education, Grandmother Tsering reminds us, is not about acquiring some kind of talent or positive quality. It is about creating and educating a positive mind with good motivation. Education is about making good people. The core of education in the Tibetan culture is not about the outside, but about the inside of a person's being.

In the old Cherokee Nation, before the Trail of Tears, keeping a good mind was so important that the annual ceremony for keeping a good clear mind and healing the mind was very similar to the ceremony for healing a physical wound, says Wilma Mankiller. "Everyone came together and spoke in public about their grievances against one another. After the Ceremony of Forgiveness, no one was to ever speak about the grievance again. The ceremony helped to keep everyone in a good frame of mind."

The Cherokee believe that actions follow thought. "If we allow ourselves to be consumed by negativity, our being becomes permeated with that and will manifest itself as negative actions. If one thinks violent and hateful thoughts, soon one will act with violence and hate," explains Wilma Mankiller. "In our world, it is very important to work with prayer and commitment to keep a positive frame of mind in our daily lives."

"Having a spiritual practice should be at the very core of the educational system," Grandmother Tsering believes. "Today the educational system is under duress. We need to learn to relate to each other with loving-kindness. Whatever religious tradition we belong to, this is a key to a good education for life."

In the Grandmothers' traditions, it is believed that children are not born with original sin but with original sanctity and are gifts from God, reflecting the balance of the mother/father principle of Creation, the source of all life. In the Lakota tradition of Grandmothers Rita and Beatrice Long Visitor Holy Dance, children are considered sacred beings. The teachings of their holy woman, White Buffalo Calf Woman, say that children have an understanding that goes beyond their years. They are the coming generation, which is why they are the most important and precious ones. In the Yupik tradition of Grandmother Rita Pitka Blumenstein, children are thought to be smarter than adults, because they are still pure beings, having just come from the Spirit World where they were recently so close to the Creator.

When the male and female energies within are in balance, our intimate relationship naturally flourishes, and any children created from that union are blessed from conception. We must not look to what we are getting or not getting from our partner, but look to ourselves for our answers to what we need, Flordemayo says. The only person who can really give you everything that you need from any relationship is yourself. "Go back to yourself and see what you are going to do for yourself first," she says. "Balancing marriage, children, work, home, and self is an incredible journey. Still, the only one you can really answer to is yourself."

When the qualities of understanding, compassion, unconditional love, and honoring the other are developed and brought to any relationship, Flordemayo says, that is when you find freedom, peace, and love in your life. "We can learn to love people for who they are, without trying to change them, by centering ourselves in the present moment. Being in the present keeps us out of past and future judgments about ourselves and others."

"Respect is the foundation of all unions between men and women," H. H. Sai Maa says. "In our intimate relationships we must honor sexuality, honor sensuality, and honor the sensitivity and heart of each other."

The Mayan teachings of Grandmother Flordemayo say that a vacuum is created in our soul when sexual energy is out of balance, and we naturally suffer depression from such a lack of soul. The soul cannot be in a relationship that has lost its connection to the sacredness of sex. Without soul within a relationship, it is impossible to see our partner as our beloved. Sacred sex allows the energy channels of each partner to always be in connection with the Divine Universe.

Yupik Grandmother Rita says an expectant mother especially needs to be nurtured and protected by her partner and those who love her, in order to help the coming child remain in a pure state. It has always been understood in the Yupik culture that the spirit of the developing infant picks up what is happening with the mother and the family while still in the womb. Stress, anger, sorrow, or frustration of the mother can then be absorbed by the developing fetus and held inside, putting the infant in a huge deficit from the beginning of life. Knowing how conscious the growing fetus is, the Yupiks teach expectant mothers how important it is to be peaceful for their child and to realize their child is already learning a great deal from them, especially about being loved. The child is also in a deficit after they are born, Grandmother Rita says, if the parents are too busy to nurture and properly train them. Making the expectant mother more aware of the great impact she has on her child even before birth sets the relationship on the right track from the beginning.

Because children are considered to be innately pure, the Grandmothers' traditions encourage modeling and rewarding virtuous behavior, rather than focusing on the restriction of bad behavior. All of us are born with spiritual values already given to us by the Creator, they say. Children therefore should be given positive reinforcement rather than being told "thou shalt not." Because children are believed to be gifts from God or the Creator, they should be treated with generosity to awaken their innate goodness and to help them attain self-realization.

Grandmother Flordemayo is grateful that she was raised translating dreams and honoring and inviting visions. As a result, she never had a question about what she came to the Earth to do. She learned from her mother to receive messages from the Spirit World, whether positive or negative, in an honoring and respectful way. The Grandmothers say that, without permission to express our dreams and visions as children, we learn to shut that part of ourselves down, making it difficult as an adult to retrieve our innate ability to see the world of Spirit. Children would benefit greatly if their parents would listen to their dreams and visions, instead of dismissing them as the product of an overly active imagination, they say. Such listening would create a closer bond and possibly help the parent access their own dreams and trust their visions again.

Children also need to be encouraged to develop strict discipline and a high regard for sharing, the Grandmothers say. They need to be encouraged not to grow lazy. For example, in the Lakota tradition, when a young girl picked her first berries or dug her first roots, she gave her harvest away to an elder for sharing, so that she would also share her future successes.

In the traditions of many of the Grandmothers, children were taught from the time they were very young not to ask why, but just to wait, watch, and listen, that when the answer finally would come to them, and it might take a year or more, it would truly be theirs. So children were taught to listen and to learn by observing—a natural teaching, since their traditional ways of life had evolved from observing what works. Because life was harsh in many ways, children were also taught out of necessity to value stoicism and to bear difficulties without complaint. Silence was also valued, because it was believed to bring out character, patience, and dignity. Love of nature, a respect for life, faith in a supreme power, and the principles of truth, generosity, honesty, equality, and kinship were instilled as guides to follow for a good life.

Children were also taught to treat everyone in the tribe as family, and they were told that all the tribal members were their mothers and fathers and grandparents. As a result, they grew up knowing they could always count on being supported and taken care of. They were also taught to be especially good to the aged and to seek out the advice of the wise ones. With such a foundation from their earliest years, children are far less likely to become troubled adolescents and teenagers, the Grandmothers say.

Without a strong sense of connection to the generations, children don't know where they've come from and so don't have any way of knowing where they are heading. "If a child doesn't have respect for elders," Grandmother Rita of Alaska says, "how can they respect themselves? Respect means to be happy and to make your elders proud of you. In my community the elders are our leaders. We learned to respect our elders like an anchor. An anchor keeps the boat safe and prevents it from drifting aimlessly all over the place."

The Grandmothers are deeply concerned with how the children of the world today are drifting and suffering so profoundly, especially with alcoholism and drugs. In the Native American cultures especially, children and teenagers have great difficulties. The traditions that have been part of their cultures for tens of thousands of years and have held the people together are no longer practiced, except by a few. The dominant culture and the media have caused young people to feel shame about who they are. But the Grandmothers have discovered that the only solution has been a return to their traditional ways. Today, young people are responding to the truths inherent in their traditional teachings and turning their lives around.

Grandmother Bernadette worries about what the children of tomorrow will become without spirituality and without the knowledge of traditional medicine that can show them the way. "Our children are in danger," she says. "Look at our youth. They are like lost orphans who are crying out. We have to begin to see many things differently. We need to build a bridge between traditional and modern medicine, so that they can come to know Spirit, instead of being given drugs as a way of solving their problems."

Children and young people need to be taught to consecrate nature, says Grandmother Maria Alice. "We must give a new answer to nature. We must teach children to respect the waters, the big trees, the mushrooms, the birds—all of life that is born here—and to realize that we are part of nature."

Grandmother Rita Long Visitor Holy Dance feels that to turn children away from such self-destruction, they have to understand that they need to take their responsibility back. "They need to believe that there are going to be better days in the future, that they can create them. They need to learn how to establish a better life, not only for their family's sake," Grandmother Rita says, "but for the sake of their own blessed children and their grandchildren to come that don't have faces yet."

Children can be empowered to make a difference in their world, Grandmother Maria Alice says. "Many years ago, children decided to raise money to buy a part of the rain forest in Costa Rica. They purchased thousands of acres of rain forest that are now protected for generations to come. There is a lot children can do to not feel helpless."

When she is working with runaway children, Grandmother Rita of Alaska stays with them and listens to them for as long as they need her. She believes the children run away because they feel they can't measure up to the expectations and standards of their parents, society, school, or friends. They haven't been allowed to learn who they are inside. "I tell them tomorrow comes the way you fear it will."

One way Grandmother Rita teaches troubled children is by having them dress the way they feel. "Show us who you are, what is going on inside you," she tells them. "Dress like a bum if you have to at first, but then learn to dress happy." Rita listens to the children's voices, not just their words, and can feel their truth.

Our problem is we tell our children what to do too much, Grandmother Rita says. "We don't accept their ways, we don't listen to them. We have to learn to listen to our children, what they need, what they want, instead of telling them they are wrong all the time." Because we don't listen, we don't know what it is they really want, she says. Not listening is why we are confused today about the direction our children are heading. Worse, we don't even listen to ourselves.

We have to make new designs for our children and for the future generations, Grandmother Agnes says. "The designs are already in the stars. The script is written, we just have to follow it. We have to open up to the spiritual energy of the design."

We have to make a prayer to God, Grandmother Clara says. "But which God can reach all the minds and hearts? The god of the box—television, because this is the greatest influence of today. It is leading our children down the wrong path, with so much distorted information."

In Brazil, there are many killings and many scenes of sex on television, Grandmother Clara says. One of the first television shows her daughter watched was about a little mouse whose home was inside a tree. Then one day, some people came and sawed the tree down. Grandmother Clara was in another room when she heard her daughter screaming. Through her tears, she asked, "Mommy, do something! Why are they doing this to this little mouse?"

"That day, I became very afraid of the power of the television," Grandmother Clara says. "My daughter was traumatized over what happened to the mouse. Imagine what would happen if she saw all the killing that was going on around the world?"

All the Grandmothers agree that the people in the media need to think clearly about the power and influence they have on young people's minds. Grandmother Bernadette feels television is the reason so much is being destroyed in our culture: respect, the family, even the forest. Children have to be taught not to be violent at home, she says, because when they come to school now they have to deal with the violence caused by their culture. Violence breeds violence.

"As a teacher by profession I ask, where are our educators in all this?" Grandmother Bernadette says. "Our children are lost. They don't know what to do. We are raising children who don't know what to do. Everything we try to do in the modern world breaks down. Before us is a very somber situation, with all the destruction that has already occurred."

No matter at what age, Helena Norberg-Hodge says, self-respect is the foundation that must be built, because it is also the foundation of respect for others. During her early years in Ladakh, she saw a people who were happier than any people she had ever known in all her travels. "Their happiness was connected to a deep sense of self-respect, which I have come to see is a cornerstone of happiness and a cornerstone of respect for others."

Helena experienced in the Ladakhi culture a love of self that was so deep that the self wasn't an issue. In Ladakh, people felt loved and respected for themselves. "It may sound exaggerated, it may sound romantic, but we can recognize from our own inner journey that when we reject our self, we reject the other," she says.

Now that Ladakh is no longer isolated but is part of the global economy, the young people especially are learning to feel dissatisfied with themselves for the first time because they are comparing themselves with the images they see of Western culture. They are becoming materialistic now that they are being targeted by the global economy to buy the right shoes, the right brands, the right stuff. They have lost self-respect. Through the impact of Western culture on the Ladakhi youth, we can see more clearly what is happening to the young people of our Western civilization. In their isolation, the people of Ladakh were able to preserve and pass down their spiritual traditions—teachings that enabled everyone in the community to live in happiness and harmony with everyone else. Now the culture is falling apart.

How did humans reach a point where they think they are more important than anyone or anything else here on our planet, Wilma Mankiller wonders. We have lost our humility and the understanding of our nonsignificance in the totality of things, she says. Before the Trail of Tears, when the Cherokee were forced to leave their land, their villages were built to reflect the shape of a particular constellation, so profound was their understanding of their place in the universe.

When we put ourselves above all else, we are no longer nourished by a sense of being in a sacred relationship with all things, the Grandmothers say. When we realize we have a direct and real relationship with the whole world and even the stars, we never have to feel lonely.

Traditional ceremonies, distinctive to each tribe, celebrated and reinforced the relationships among all tribal members in indigenous cultures. For example, Wilma Mankiller says that once a year in each of the Cherokee villages in the Southeast, a central fire would be built and an all-night ceremony would be held. Before attending the ceremony, every person was asked to put the fire out in their own homes. Then, after the sacred ceremony, each person would take a coal from the central fire and relight their own fires from the central fire. The ceremony kept the people together and helped them to share not just a geographic space but a worldview and a sense of community. The ceremony reminded the people that they lived in reciprocal relationships with each other.

When the "family fire" is not kept burning, our whole social order begins to decay and fall into disorder.

In the Grandmothers' traditions, ceremonies are considered a very important factor in keeping the people together. Throughout the world, there are hundreds of seasonal ceremonies conducted by indigenous peoples, the Grandmothers say. For example, every spring in Utah, the Utes have a Bear Dance to shake off the effects of a long winter and to prepare the people for what is ahead. The Cherokee have an annual Green Corn ceremony to celebrate the ripening of the corn. Ceremonies have been held since the beginning of time, Wilma Mankiller says, to celebrate the sacred relationship between the people and the land.

"Peace is paramount in these ceremonies," Wilma says. "The main difference between our people and the world around us is our understanding of our sacred relationship with the Earth, the environment, and the natural world, and our resulting gratitude and respect."

To the Cherokee and many other of the Grandmothers' tribes, every day is considered a good day, even when plans are upset because of rain.

"You just accept the rain and go on," Wilma Mankiller says. "Our people know about acceptance and contentment."

The Cherokee don't feel that they have to be happy all the time, Wilma says. Happiness depends on something outside ourselves and so is always in flux. Peace of mind, however, creates a deeper sense of contentment. For the Cherokee, as with other indigenous peoples, the seasonal cycles of ceremonies are to bring peace of mind and healing, and the rest is left to the Creator. "With peace of mind, you can deal with almost anything," Wilma explains.

The Cherokee people may seem poor, Wilma says, "but we feel we are actually the wealthiest people in the world, because we still have our languages, our ceremonies, our traditional medicines, and most important, our sense of interdependence. We have a commitment to one another and a sense of community, of clan, of nation. We still care about one another. The people who are most respected in our community are not the people who have accumulated great personal wealth or attained a high position. We are involved in a reciprocal system. We help one another. When the white people came to this continent, most would have died if the Indians had not been willing to share their ways."

This attitude of responsibility for one another is something we must develop to ensure our survival, Grandmother Tsering says. "The focus of the world must not be solely upon creating material goods and amassing wealth. We must begin thinking about the peace and well-being of individuals all over the world. My teacher, the Dalai Lama, does not just seek peace for our country of Tibet, but desires peace for the whole planet."

During this time of unprecedented planetary evolution, where time is more accelerated than at any time in recorded history, our choices will determine what our world will become, the Grandmothers remind us. We must be willing to move out of habitual choices based on fear, isolation, and survival, and move into proactive choices to heal, grow, and expand our consciousness, both as individuals and globally. Because we are all in relationship with each other and all things, the low level of energy created by the emotions of fear, shame, defensiveness, judgment, resistance, and greed bring down the energy of everyone and everything around us. Instead, we need to develop an instinctive ability to reach for the higher-energy responses to situations, like love, gratitude, and hope.

The spirit behind our intentions is what changes the world and our lives, the Grandmothers say. When we begin to understand we are much more than our needs and desires, our personalities and egos, that we come from the stars and that our souls are ever evolving, then we meet each other at a different place. We bring the unity inherent in Creation to all our relations. We were born sacred beings, the Grandmothers remind us. Our problems come from forgetting that, and from forgetting that all the Creator asked of us was to love one another and to be stewards of His Creation. Our hearts and minds need to become full of yearning for the good will of all people and of our Mother Earth.

"Nothing belongs to us," Grandmother Rita from Alaska explains. "Even the Earth does not belong to the Earth. We are all here to serve the universe."

Our Mother Earth

OUR SMALL BLUE PLANET, valiantly existing on the outer edge of the Milky Way galaxy among countless billions of stars and suns of other planets and other galaxies, has nurtured and protected humanity, providing for all of our needs, for tens of thousands, if not millions of years. Our waters are Her blood; the rain forest that is our pharmacy is Her lungs. The rocks we use for building are Her bones. Yet most of humanity never thinks to bless and thank Her, much less repay Her.

Mother Earth is a conscious, alive, and responsive being, the Grandmothers say, ever evolving within the divine order of the cosmos—a goddess in Her own right. When speaking about how our sacred waters are too polluted to drink, how the Amazon rain forest will soon be gone, how much of "our Mother's face" is paved over and has garbage heaped upon it, the Grandmothers weep. They feel the Earth's suffering as if the pain were their own.

In less than one hundred years, driven by our desire for wealth, comfort, and material goods, we have exploited and depleted vast resources, upsetting the delicate natural balance of our planet. Respect for our interdependence is cruelly lacking, and we have lost all humility before Creation. Because of the arrogance, greed, and indifference of so many of the Earth's children, we have reached the end of living and the beginning of survival, the Grandmothers say. Self-indulgence and delusional materialism have brought us to the brink of self-destruction.

"We have traded the welfare of future generations for immediate profit," Grandmother Agnes says. "Because of spiritual blindness, people look to the bottom line, rather than looking at life."

"Our planet is sick from the never-ending ravages of people, pollution, deforestation, abusive power, jealousy, and hatred," Grandmother Bernadette says. "As the Earth increasingly suffers, we have become more and more disoriented and have lost our way."

Horrific wars have transformed people, destroying what is human and traumatizing generations to come. Such violence unleashes famine, poverty, and diseases and causes the death of ideas and culture. Children are orphaned and families forever separated. Just as a tree in Africa responds to the felling of a tree in the Amazon, a single bomb falling on Iraq reverberates throughout the world and out into the universe, changing all of us forever and changing the living consciousness of our planet as well. The web of destruction has been as intricately woven as the web of life.

"Life is very precious. Every blade of grass is our relative," Grandmother Agnes reminds us. "Every one-legged—the Tree People—needs our voice. The animal kingdom and the swimmers in the water need our voice. They are crying out for help."

In a single tree, there are four or five ecosystems, Grandmother Agnes explains. Yet on highways around the world, mighty trees are chained together onto log trucks, ancient giants heading for chipping mills, many to be shipped to Japan, where they are transformed into cardboard boxes to hold the stereos, televisions, and other electronic equipment for eager consumers.

We are all connected to all things, the Grandmothers remind us. What we do to the Earth and to the inhabitants of the Earth, we do to ourselves. Some of our own nobility of spirit is lost when we are not touched to the core by senseless, selfish exploitation of nature's beauty.

Reflecting what is happening to the kingdoms of nature, children coming into the world now deal with pollution while in the womb from the toxins in their mother's system, Grandmother Flordemayo says. The first breast milk an infant receives is tainted with the chemicals the mother carries in her body from the creams, shampoos, and cosmetics she uses, not to mention the effects of pollution in her environment.

The greatest tragedy of all is that the devastating results of our disrespectful attitudes, which will become increasingly apparent, could have been completely avoided. The future, just like the past, is our collective choice.

The Earth has been warning us for a long time, the Grandmothers explain. Now we are being forced to listen. Increasingly destructive natural events such as enormous hurricanes, endless numbers of tornadoes, terrible flooding, and devastating earthquakes are the planet's natural response to the necessity of restoring the delicate balance that is required to unconditionally nourish all life. Prophecies speak about the cleansing of the Earth at this time. Humanity must now be awakened to the destruction we have caused to vast areas of our planet, before it is too late and all is destroyed.

The Ancient Ones told humanity that it is our job to care for the animals and all the kingdoms of nature, the Grandmothers say. In the creation myths of the Grandmothers' traditions, it is said that in the beginning, wisdom and knowledge were gained from the animals, that the Creator did not speak directly to humanity. He showed himself through the beasts. Through observing all the kingdoms of nature and the stars and the sun and the moon, humanity was to humbly learn how to live on this planet. Everything on the Earth was created for a purpose. For every disease there was a cure in the plant kingdom, and every person was born with a mission, the Grandmothers say.

"We especially need the animals to keep the balance," Grandmother Agnes explains. "If we don't take care of our animal kingdom, we ourselves are dying faster than we think."

ANIMALS ARE NOW HAVING TO COME DOWN FROM the mountains and from the forests to the cities and into homes in the suburbs because there isn't enough food. Black bears are entering peoples' homes looking for food, because their natural resources are gone. In the Everglades, where condominiums are going up, canals are being built to allow development, and these canals are having a significant impact on Everglades wildlife, especially the alligators.

"Alligators never lived in canals," Grandmother Agnes says. "So they are climbing up onto the highways and getting run over, or else are found sitting on a porch and the people can't get their doors open. The alligators have a right to live as much as we do."

The creation story of Grandmother Agnes's people, which is similar to many other indigenous peoples' creation stories, states that the Creator created men and women to take care of His Creation, which was why He was giving them a brain and with that brain the power to reason. The Creator gave us our gifts to be a voice for the voiceless, Grandmother Agnes explains. Humans were told to use all the gifts of nature in moderation and to keep all things in balance.

"We have walked away from these teachings," she says. "Now, the one-leggeds—the Tree People—the creepy crawlers, the winged ones, the four-leggeds, all are running out of space, and their environment is being encroached upon. There are no controlled burnings of the forest for the Tree People as in the old days. The waters are too polluted in places to sustain the lives of so many of the plants and animals. We need to do a better job."

In her travels, Grandmother Agnes has seen what clear-cut logging has done. There are no more big trees to hold the moisture down for the little shoots, and so they die. The old people of her community would say that if you take the trees off of the top of the mountains, you change the climate, because the ancient trees are the ones that call the wind and the rain. "Wind patterns are being destroyed; things that used to grow to hold the ground are being pulled up," Grandmother Agnes explains. "Paving has caused erosion all over the lands."

Each part of the world has treasures of plant and animal life that grow nowhere else, yet are being destroyed to build commercial property, homes, and roads. The wildlife have no voice with which to defend themselves, the Grandmothers say, and are being lost to us forever. To indulge our whims and fantasies, we have forced species of plants to grow where they were never meant to be. Wild animals are taken from their natural environment and forced to live where they do not belong. The impact on their collective spirits has impacted our own collective spirit. Now, wherever we travel in America, every town looks the same because of

Mother Earth is a conscious, alive, and responsive being— a goddess in Her own right.

the generic strip malls and buildings that are replacing the original beauty and unique character of each place. Just as the indigenous peoples have always known, when we lose our land we are no longer who we say we are.

Because of their intimacy with the land, native peoples are aware that there are places on the Earth where spiritual energy is particularly strong. Just as our bodies have meridians and an auric field, so too does the Earth. Ley lines are energy lines that pass through sacred sites and places of power. These energy vortexes are similar to acupuncture points and chakras in the human body. These places on the Earth are set aside for ceremony and ritual by native peoples, as they are considered sacred. However, commercial values too often supersede spiritual values in today's world. For instance, the Alaskan pipeline was laid through some sacred places of the native peoples with no understanding of the true damage caused. Those sacred places heal us. They are our medicine, whether or not we are natives, and we all are violated along with the land.

"Just because it doesn't have a steeple or a church, they swear to God that those places aren't sacred," Grandmother Agnes says. "That is spiritual blindness."

Many of our prophecies about the Purification Times have already come to pass, the Grandmothers say. We can only wait and see if the future ones will come true. We must pray to change the dark around, pray to change our way of thinking.

"From what I have been told," Luisah Teish explains, "the Earth has given us enough food, enough water, plants, beautiful animals, enough wonderful people. None of us ever really need be poor, if we can get control of those who are greedy. Then we can see that materially everyone is already rich." To get to that point, we must first connect with our own rich spirits, she says, which will automatically cause us to take actions to share all we have been given.

With each passing year, ever-quickening vibrations intensify the pressure for all of us to become more conscious of our true spiritual nature. When we live from higher vibrations of love, gratitude, and generosity, we will match the changing vibrations of the Earth and will not be as affected as She shakes off the negativity that we have inflicted upon Her, and as we shake off the materialistic prison we have created for ourselves. We will begin to measure our wealth not by how much we accumulate, but by how much we give.

WHEN WE BEGIN TO UNDERSTAND the divinity, the cosmology of all life, we will no longer take our beautiful planet for granted, the Grandmothers say. In these days, when the prophecies are being fulfilled, we are the ones who will determine whether or not we will destroy our Mother Earth and ourselves. Each one of us must decide now whether or not to live wisely and with a selfless love for the benefit of all. Will we choose to awaken to our higher consciousness in the face of dramatic Earth changes? Will we choose life?

Grandmother Agnes is asked to pray all over the world where rivers or land are threatened with pollution or development. Just as with the Salmon Ceremony, her prayers have been effective. As the numbers of salmon have increased each year, we have learned that, when the water is reclaimed for the salmon, we have at the same time reclaimed the soil, the plants, and other species of the ecosystem, restoring full health for our children and future generations as well.

Dwelling, whether in our own home, in our town, or on our beautiful planet, is not primarily about inhabiting, but taking care of and creating that space within which something can come into its own and flourish. It takes time and ritual for real dwelling, the Grandmothers say. Ecological systems are far too complex for even the greatest scientists to fully understand or figure out how to control. So we must have respect instead of knowledge and honor the mystery, which is what will actually bring us further in our understanding of our individual and collective place on this Earth, an understanding that science could never reach. In fact, the true essence of civilization is learned through observing with humility our true place within all of Creation.

"Humanity must enter a reconciliation with nature if we wish to create a new reality, a new alliance," Grandmother Bernadette says. "We must learn the essential and mysterious language of nature that is always speaking to us, the language the great initiates have always understood."

Change will not be created by passing laws or developing technology, the Grandmothers say. What needs to be developed is a deeper, more personal sense of connection with the Earth and our place on it.

One way to create a deeper and more personal sense of connection is by holding rituals, ceremonies, and festivals. Ritual and ceremony are sophisticated social and spiritual technologies, refined by indigenous peoples over many thousands of years, to celebrate and nurture the world order of a particular place. Seasonal rituals and ceremonies speak to the whole community, which includes the plants, animals, and soil of a place and not just the human relationships.

Ritual and ceremony not only create respect for our interdependence with the natural environment but open worlds so that we can actually find ourselves within nature, an essential key to creating sustainable culture and restoring nature's balance. A proper relationship to the land and the natural world requires the whole of our being, the Grandmothers say. We can't just view our world from the rational, practical left side of the brain but must connect in a way that feels greater than ourselves. We must engage the intuitive, imaginative right side of the brain with celebration, music, art, dance, games, and mythology. We are then able to connect the conscious with the unconscious, keeping open an essential connection with ourselves and driving out negativity. Ritual is supposed to take us out of ourselves. Afterward, we are not meant to be in the same place psychologically or spiritually as before the ritual.

RITUAL ENGAGES THE SPIRIT OF A PLACE, a circuit of energy in which the entire cosmos participates. With a renewed connection to the spiritual powers found in the unseen world that ritual and ceremony tap into, we grow stronger in our dormant wisdom and become conscious ecologists. We learn to know just how much we can take from a place before the natural balance is thrown off, because this energy flows among all things, including humanity. Rituals and ceremony are a form of prayer, and our prayers for the world are our greatest contribution to its healing and rebirth, the Grandmothers say.

Ritual and ceremony require a historical, cultural, and community context. Most places on Earth have been inhabited by indigenous cultures, before they were driven away by what has been called civilization. Research can reveal ancient rituals, ceremonies, and celebrations

Increasingly destructive natural events are the planet's way of restoring the delicate balance that is required to nourish all life.

that are still specific and true to a place, and that can connect us with the mythology and intensify our participation with our environment. Rituals have many layers of meaning and truth. Essential to successful rituals and ceremony is a sense of aliveness: something new needs to be created out of the ancient rites for ritual and celebration to be engaging.

In Tibet, Grandmother Tsering says, their traditional rituals and ceremonies kept the lives of the people very open and spacious. The environment was often honored with rituals and celebrations. "We believed there were deities in our environment," she says. "We would never dig in our mountains, for instance, because we had great respect for them."

In the tradition of indigenous tribes around the world, countries, states, schools, and universities have an animal, flower, or tree as a symbol. In the Native American traditions, totem animals were selected from their environment to symbolize power, goodness, or an admired quality or character trait to aspire to. Often, the totem animal was considered a teacher as well and provided protection. Usually, the animal was the one on whom the tribe depended the most, and always it symbolized interdependence. It was believed quite possible that animals could understand humans better than humans understood them.

The salmon is the totem animal for the North Pacific Rim. It was also the totem for some Celtic tribes of Old Europe. Besides being the primary source of food, the salmon reminded the people of the vastness and unity of the world. By becoming one with the salmon, the people could acquire the qualities of nurturing and courage and know at a deeper level the meaning of sacred relations.

According to legend, the buffalo were the gift of White Buffalo Calf Woman. The Sioux depended on the buffalo for food, clothing, and housing, and so the buffalo were considered holy to the people. Life, death, and resurrection were the themes reenacted in their ritual and ceremony, reflecting a profound understanding of and reverence for life. Tragically, in less than ten years, hundreds of thousands of buffalo were slaughtered for sport by encroaching settlers, pioneers who obviously had no concept of the sacred oneness of Creation.

"Disdain and rejection of the Other," Grandmother Bernadette explains, "signal the practice of all forms of discrimination."

As Earth's children, we are to love one another, the Grandmothers remind us. And we must show great respect for all of Creation. Wherever there is discrimination, even among religions, there is a complete lack of understanding of true spirituality and a lessening of hope for the continuation of life on Earth.

One way to break through to a new level of understanding is to look within and honor a strong attraction to a particular wild animal, a kind of tree or plant, or a particular place on the Earth. All people have their own personal totems. In the Grandmothers' traditions, it is taught that people must make themselves worthy of that toward which they are attracted, so that they might have dreams or visions that might purify and clarify their lives. Study an animal. Learn its innocent ways and appreciate its complexity. In that study, we can learn about ourselves by understanding what it is we are attracted to. Is it a quality we need to develop, or one we already have but need to honor? The traditions teach that animals want to communicate with people, but people must make the effort. Such a practice alone can create a spiritual awakening and bring greater consciousness to all things.

We can make a difference, but there isn't much time, the Grandmothers say. We must stop pollution now. It is time for there to be no more hunger in our world. There should never be any hunger. The United States especially needs to learn how wrong it is to throw so much away. We must join those who are already fighting for our Mother Earth, fighting for the betterment of all our lives here on our beautiful planet. Together we have the power to make a difference, the Grandmothers say.

Inner-city dwellers can be encouraged to continue to transform old empty lots into gardens, says Louisah Teish. Till the soil and see what wants to grow. See how the birds arrive. Inviting and participating with nature in community gardens and parks can drive negativity out of neighborhoods everywhere. In some cities, trees and vegetation are being planted on rooftops of skyscrapers to invite healthy conditions for the people. We can take care of our local water, for instance, by making sure that farmers are not polluting rivers and streams with what they are feeding the cattle or with the drugs they are giving them. We can do a better job taking care of the land, the air, and the waters. We can all make a difference wherever we live, when we have clear and balanced minds, a full heart, and a willing spirit, the Grandmothers say. We are facing a long road, and we need to be conscious every day.

"We forget that everything comes from Mother Earth, even the clothes on our backs," Grandmother Agnes says. "We are in denial about what we are doing. We must see ourselves in the whole context. We all breathe the same air. Let's make it clean and healthy."

The Earth and the elements have the capacity to mend themselves. That life is a circle is a sacred law. Hope springs when people choose to learn and change their ways. We can regenerate the land with a return to reciprocity and the sacred ceremonies. Modern science is the grandchild, not the father, of ritual work. Though quantum physics is only proving it now, moving energy through ritual has been used to heal for many thousands of years. There was a time, the Grandmothers remind us, when all of our ancestors revered the Earth and used ritual to maintain the Earth's balance. It is important to reclaim that reverence and gratitude and reconstruct what has been lost.

The true essence of civilization is learned through observing with humility our true place within all of Creation.

We have to be careful about how we treat even a blade of grass, Grandmother Agnes says. We need to understand that the trees give us the ability to live on this planet, because we breathe the air that comes from and is cleansed by them. Most people don't even know the history of the ground they walk upon, she says.

The old people used to tell the people to go to the oceans or the rivers or the streams and call up the water spirits for healing and rebalancing, the Grandmothers say. When you are feeling low, go to the Mother. Even a shower or a bath makes a difference. Now there is scientific language that explains what the Ancient Ones always knew, that negative ions from water have an impact on the brain that serves as an antidepressant.

We are not the greatest or smartest culture that ever existed on this *Our* planet, Luisah Teish reminds us. Evolution is not linear, it is a spiral. *Mother* "There have been people on this planet far more intelligent than we *Earth* are," she says. "What we have to do is overcome our indoctrination."

All of us are connected to the whales, the wolves, the polar bears, to all of Creation. We should all be praying that drilling doesn't impact the great caribou migration patterns, because we too will be hurt, the Grandmothers say. When we feel a magnetic pull, it is an awakening that we are intensely connected to something happening in nature that is vibrating through our body.

We must teach our children a new way, in order to ensure that future generations will experience the beauty and abundance the Creator has given to us. We must humbly pray to the rocks, the trees, the sky, the mountains, the sacred waters, the birds, and the animals to help us, to give us their power to help us with all of our struggles, to help us to be of service and help us to heal.

Oppression

OPPRESSION was legitimized by various medieval papal bulls and edicts, which were signed by Pope Alexander while Christopher Columbus was exploring the New World, a world new to the Europeans but ancient to the highly civilized people who had been living in the Americas, Africa, and Oceania for tens of thousands of years.

The relationship between nation-states and tribal peoples around the world rests on the foundation of these "doctrines of conquest" that justified the seizing of all lands and properties of "heathen peoples." These papal edicts granted dominion to European nations over lands that had been occupied by tribal peoples for thousands of years and set into motion a disastrous chain of events that ultimately resulted in the outright theft of entire continents from indigenous peoples worldwide.

While these papal bulls and edicts were written over five hundred years ago, they have yet to be rescinded and remain the spiritual, legal, and moral foundation for the exercise of jurisdiction over tribal nations by nation-states today. The justification for doctrines of conquest has grown like a cancer in the world and set into motion not just the rape and pillage of indigenous peoples around the world but also the plundering of the resources of weak and vulnerable people everywhere up until the present day, the Grandmothers say.

Now, like those explorers and pioneers who swept across the Americas, ransacking environments, decimating cultures, and nearly wiping out the entire population of indigenous peoples, materialism promoted by the global economy is wiping out democracy, community, cultural diversity, and spirituality. What was done to the indigenous peoples around the globe in the name of colonialism, which stems from the same belief in entitlement as the doctrines of conquest, is being done to all of us in our "rape-and-run" economy.

"Unchecked materialism has caused environmental degradation, perilous climate changes, war and terrorism, extreme poverty, and nuclear proliferation," Helena Norberg-Hodge says. "We must begin to save ourselves from the worst consequences of our own behavior."

Even the politicians will continue to see their power shrinking at the expense of giant transnational corporations, Helena says. Transnational institutions can overpower any government. Companies like Halliburton have the power to move into Iraq after the U.S. bombing and even New Orleans after the devastation of Hurricane Katrina, taking away the ability of local citizens to rebuild their own cities. The corporate economy robs us of access to our own skills and our own resources. Outsiders in both Iraq and New Orleans have usurped the power of local citizens to rebuild, in much the same way that native peoples have been stripped of their lands, and with the same potential result looming. People in their homelands will no longer be able to be who they say they are.

Destruction of our integrity is now more subtle, says Helena. Wealth is not even with the nations but with the "rootless casino of the financial markets."

Without finding a new way of seeing and being that resonates with the ancient and time-proven Earth-based traditions and practices of indigenous peoples, we will not survive, the Grandmothers say.

Grandmother Agnes is a descendent of the Trail of Tears, the forced march of Native Americans from their original lands. Her people no longer make their lives on the land they believed the Creator had given to them to care for. In her part of the country, it was the miners who ran the Native Americans off their land.

"When September 11 happened, it was said by everyone that that was the worst tragedy to happen in the U.S.," Grandmother Agnes says. "Oh no, the treatment of the First Nation people of this land is the biggest tragedy and disgrace in this country."

Cheyenne Grandmother Margaret Behan's earliest memory is as a five-year-old living with her grandparents in a two-room house. Every morning, her grandmother would yell out, "Do not forget the white people killed us!"

"As a little girl, I didn't understand," Grandmother Margaret says. "I was alive, not dead."

Five generations away from the Sand Creek Massacre, Grandmother Margaret is an example of generational trauma, caused by oppression, war, and violence. From her example, we can see how the people of Iraq will still be dealing with the impact of the war five generations from now, how so much of humanity suffers and will continue to suffer from the trauma created by wars and oppression past and present.

The fact that the Cheyenne were the last of the Indian nations to move to the reservation, that the people fought to the end, redeemed some sense of pride for Margaret's uncles and is an important part of the story of their people that Margaret now tells her grandchildren. Margaret has spared few details of the reality of how the soldiers came and killed their ancestors. Her grandchildren can't imagine why the soldiers would do such things.

"I tell them that the soldiers wanted the land, and our skin was not white," Margaret says. "I don't want to tell them the very difficult and ugly images, but I have to because the story is true. Soldiers cut our great-great-grandmothers' breasts off. Why pick women and children to mutilate and kill? Because we are weak and vulnerable. The genocide of my people is not something I can just 'get over' by going to a shrink. There are no quick answers."

The massacre of their people at Wounded Knee, the shooting of babies in utero that happened there, is still a part of a legacy of trauma for the Lakota Nation. Grandmothers Rita and Beatrice grew up hearing the stories of how the soldiers would cut the babies from their mothers' wombs, then toss the babies in the air and shoot them. "These children were sacred, and still they did this to them," Grandmother Rita says.

"Many things were brought to this country from many nations," Grandmother Rita says. "The most terrible have been the alcohol, the bad smoke, the bad medicine. Our children and grandchildren are not remembering anything. They are too far gone on drugs and alcoholism."

Successive generations after the genocide of the native peoples have been weakened from the trauma, but also from the fact that the DNA of native peoples does not have the capacity to withstand drugs and alcohol.

"Among our possible future leaders are children who suffer from fetal alcohol syndrome," Grandmother Rita says. "They will never fulfill their potential because of the bad medicines. Our greatest challenge is changing that for our children and for the future generations."

Returning to our culture of origin helps us regain our resilience. What keeps us connected are our stories and contact, says Alice Walker. When those go, we lose our resilience. Especially when young people come to understand their past, their lineage, they are naturally more re-silient and much less likely to abuse drugs and alcohol, to take sexual risks, or have multiple illnesses. If they know any story at all, they are more resilient than if those stories are lost. Even if those stories are of generations of violence or loss, they will still be more resilient and less likely to abuse their children. Indigenous peoples need to go back and find the rest of their stories, she says.

The other holocaust to indigenous peoples was the Atlantic slave trade, in which twelve million mostly West Africans were captured and enslaved in the Americas.

"Black people have ancestors that survived the slave ships and lived through plantation life," Luisah Teish says. "They've continued despite hangings and tarrings and featherings. I tell young people to call on their ancestors to surround them, whenever they are afraid. These strong ancestors will make a circle around them."

The United States was founded on violence, Gloria Steinem says. The violence on television today is connected to our origins. "This country is like a child," she says. "A child who's had a trauma tends to re-peat the trauma until the trauma is understood and dealt with. We all have a lot to gain by talking openly about what was done to the native people, who were only welcoming when we arrived on their shores."

The reward for facing the atrocities would be access to the wisdom of Native Americans, Gloria says. "The lack of community we feel, the

lack of spirituality. We have much to gain, but we first must face the violence and dig it out."

Wars have existed for a long time, Grandmother Maria Alice says. "I believe the idea of war comes into man's mind when he becomes far from God. He thinks he can be more than his brothers and sisters, rather than believing we are all equal and all creatures of God. He wants to be more than or above the plants, the animals, and the water. This kind of man is in competition with the Creator. He thinks he can be the Creator. This is my understanding of what generates wars and oppression. Peace comes from the opposite of this kind of thinking. When we can feel we are brothers and sisters with all the creatures and with the beauty of God, we will know peace."

"It is easy to make war," Grandmother Beatrice says. "Jealousy, greed, and bad feelings about people of other colors are difficult feelings to get rid of. To have peace is a great struggle. We believe that to have peace we must choose to have our thoughts be truthful and good. Despite the genocide that was done against our people and to others all over the United States, our people are still praying for peace. Our red people carry a peace pipe and pray for peace with our peace pipes. We Sun Dance and do vision quests. We practice the seven sacred rites. And we pray for all four colors of man to pray with us."

We cannot break the cycles of violence around the world without also healing the perpetrators, the Grandmothers say. We must build on the pain of the past with honesty, even honesty with our children. We can't pretend the suffering did not exist. But we must build on the pain of the past without giving in to it, they say. Anger can be transformative. Only when we give voice to the pain, whether we are the oppressed or the oppressor, can the healing then begin. Only by dealing with the past can we see the effects of our actions in the present.

"As a Grandmother speaking for my grandchildren and for the next seven generations, I feel we must see how we are all mirrors for each other," Grandmother Margaret says. "White people ask me how I can love them, and I say because I can see myself in you."

Historically, the erosion of cultural integrity was a conscious goal of colonial developers and missionaries. For Native Americans and many indigenous peoples around the world, school was the prime coercive instrument for tampering with underlying core values, the Grandmothers say. Children were not permitted to speak their native language or practice any of their native traditions while attending school. They were most often boarded nine months out of the year to lessen family influence and further weaken ties with their culture.

"The schools were highly effective in destroying self-esteem, fostering new needs, creating dissatisfaction, and disrupting traditional cultures," Helena says.

Oppression continues. Erosion of cultures, even our dominant one, is taken over by television today, Helena says. Though not physically brutal in its methods, the scale and effects can be more devastating. Just like the missionary schools around the world, young people are targeted by advertisers because their minds are still pliable.

We cannot break the cycles of violence around the world without also healing the perpetrators.

Television and the Internet have intensified the pressure to buy products in order to conform to the homogenized culture of the global village. Though not physical, violence is perpetrated on the soul, nevertheless. More and more young people, as well as adults, are feeling shame about who they are if they don't conform to the Western ideal of beauty (and most people don't). As we become increasingly disconnected from our souls, we seek the material world or drugs in an attempt to fill the emptiness.

The native peoples of the Americas are now generations removed from their original trauma, as are the African Americans. They still experience the perpetuation of their suffering. We witness what the loss of great civilizations like those of the Mayans, Incas, and Aztecs, as well as the many Native American tribes, means to humanity, by watching what Tibet has been going through right before our eyes, if we would look, the Grandmothers say.

In the short span of time since the Chinese occupation of 1950, the ancient and amazing civilization and ecosystems of Tibet are facing extinction. From a tiny country so spiritual that it had thousands of monasteries and nunneries filled with monks and nuns from nearly every family, today's Chinese-occupied Tibet no longer permits Tibetans to practice their religion within their own borders. Since the invasion, over six thousand monasteries, nunneries, temples, and shrines have been destroyed. As a direct result of the Chinese occupation, 1.2 million Tibetans have died as victims of warfare, forced labor, executions, torture, suicide, and famine. More than 100,000 Tibetan refugees, including the Dalai Lama and Grandmother Tsering, barely escaped to India and Nepal.

Tibetan women, including Grandmother Tsering, are at the forefront of the Tibetan people's struggle for independence and self-determination. It was the women who originally planned and led the major uprising of 1959 against the Chinese occupation. They continue their fight, despite being constantly subjected to the most degrading and inhumane treatment, including sexual abuse and torture of a kind almost beyond imagination. According to the Tibet Justice Center, electric cattle prods and attack dogs are still frequently used on the women as well as the men. As with the Cheyenne, Sioux, and many other native women, Tibetan women too have had their breasts cut off. Still the women's commitment to fighting for Tibetan independence endures.

Exiles know that it is up to those who escaped to preserve the Tibetan culture and their language, but with each passing year Tibet is becoming increasingly lost, Grandmother Tsering says. To find work in their own country, Tibetans are required to speak Chinese, a difficult language that takes a long time to perfect. So, many Tibetans have no hope of finding work. Traditional Tibetan dress is banned. Cut off from their essential roots, the culture and traditions that evolved naturally from their land, Tibetans are losing their resilience. The soul of a whole country, one of the most spiritual on the planet, will soon be forever lost. Now only 30 percent of Tibet is inhabited by Tibetans, and the percentage will decrease when the new railroad China is building to link China to Tibet is completed (projected completion date, 2007).

Since Tibet is not their native land, the Chinese don't have the same feeling for Tibet as the Tibetans. In the mountains, once so revered, the Chinese are burying radioactive waste. The Earth is being harmed, and Tibet is becoming a poisoned place. Instead of being able to nurture the people there as has been the case for thousands of years, Mother Earth is a force of death, with no way to transform the danger. The Tibetans fear that the world doesn't even care.

"To keep the Tibetan culture alive," Grandmother Tsering says, "we grandmothers who still remember must teach our children and grandchildren, or a whole beautiful culture, with its own unique teachings, will be lost to humanity."

The outcasts are lucky, Grandmother Tsering believes. Those who escaped the Chinese invasion and oppression of Tibet can still speak their language and practice their customs. Without their land or resources, they do the best they can. The Tibetan way of dressing and its dances, language, and culture are all being preserved by the exiles.

Whereas the tragedy of Tibet exemplifies the inhumane treatment of indigenous cultures around the world for the last five hundred years, the story of Ladakh serves as a mirror for what is being lost to all of us as we are being moved by huge multinational corporations toward looking at the world as one global village. Helena witnessed firsthand the insidiousness of the global economy with its covert oppression and has been trying to get the message out for the last thirty years. Because she had the privilege to observe Ladakh before it was invaded by the modern world, she was able to observe the last truly free people on the planet.

What Helena encountered twelve thousand feet high on the Tibetan plateau, living in one of the most difficult environments on the planet, with only glacial mountain water to irrigate the desert and a four-month growing period, was a people and a culture that was still free, a people that had been able to develop, change, and evolve, but on their own terms, according to their own values and their own needs, despite difficult conditions. They escaped becoming slaves and being put on a plantation to grow cotton for Europe, or having their whole region turned into a coffee country, or a tin country, or whatever else was needed for the central European empire, Helena says.

The Ladakhi architecture was magnificent—three-story-high buildings, all painted white, with beautiful carved wooden balconies. There was no waste or pollution, and crime was virtually nonexistent. The

women wore jewelry of turquoise, gold, silver, coral, and pearls from all
over the world, which showed they had lived well above subsistence.

"There was wealth, more than was necessary. In effect, the jewels were a type of bank," Helena explains. "I was astounded. Villagers provided for their basic needs without money. I had never encountered anything like this in all my worldly travels. What it proved to me was that the growing poverty around the world was a product of an expansionist, global, colonial economy and that expansionism is the root of so much of the poverty, violence, and the loss of community and family we see today."

When Helena first visited Ladakh, the only thing the people needed to import from outside their region was salt. Now part of the global economy, Helena sees that the people of Ladakh are finding themselves more and more dependent, for even their most basic needs, on an economic system that is controlled by forces far from their own lands and that are beyond their control, like oil prices, transportation networks, and the fluctuating world markets.

"They are at the mercy of people's decisions, who do not even know Ladakh exists," Helena says, "and their local economy is crumbling as their influence and power over their village-scale economy has been reduced to zero. They have become a part of a global economy of six billion, which requires them to produce more and more in order to have enough income to buy what they used to produce for themselves."

The result, Helena has observed over the years, have been a growing insecurity and competitiveness, even leading to ethnic conflict, among a once-secure and cooperative people. "A range of social problems has appeared almost overnight, including crime, family breakup, and homelessness," Helena explains. "As the Ladakhis have become separated from the land, the awareness of the limits of local resources has dimmed. Pollution is on the increase, and the population is growing at unsustainable rates."

Helena does not feel that Ladakh before the intrusion of the world was a utopia. There were what Westerners would call problems, such as illiteracy, and what most of the world would call substandard living conditions. But the people had their soul.

"As they lose the sense of security and identity that springs from deep, long-lasting connections to people and place, the Ladakhis are beginning to develop doubts about who they are," Helena explains. "The images they get from outside tell them to be different, to own more, to buy more and thus be 'better' than they are. The previously strong, outgoing women of Ladakh have been replaced by a new generation—unsure of themselves and desperately concerned about their appearance."

Ladakhis now wear wristwatches they can't read and apologize for having no electricity in their homes which, when they were first introduced to the idea, the people laughed at.

"Ironically, modernization, which is so often associated with the triumph of individualism, has produced a loss of individuality and a growing sense of personal insecurity, as people feel pressured to conform and live up to an idealized image," Helena observes. "By contrast, in the traditional village, where everyone wore essentially the same clothes and looked the same to the casual observer, there was more freedom to relax. As part of a close-knit community, people felt secure enough to be themselves.

"Self-respect is the foundation of respect for others," Helena believes. "Self-love is the foundation for the love of others. What I experienced in this culture was the love of self was so deep that the self wasn't an issue. I'm speaking of a way of life where people feel loved and accepted, and through that are able to love and accept others in a way that people who feel marginalized and undervalued can't."

Grandmother Margaret grew up in a family where some members could pass for white. Her aunt liked hanging out at the air force base and wanted to be like the white people, drinking alcohol and smoking cigarettes. In fact, she wanted to be a white woman, Margaret says. This made an impression on Margaret and, when she became a young woman, she too wanted to wear high heels and drink like the white women. But Margaret soon became an alcoholic and went on to marry and have three children, before finally coming to terms with the root cause of her alcoholism.

Because of undiagnosed oppression and generational trauma as perpetrators of inhumane treatment of indigenous peoples, few who have oppressor ancestry are able to react with courage to help the oppressed, the Grandmothers believe.

"Each individual, as they live within their own country, is naturally focused on the interests of that particular country," Grandmother Tsering says, "and they don't think about the world in general getting increasingly dangerous."

Our world situation is not entirely hopeless, but we must take back our lives at the local level, Helena believes, especially at the economic level. "Real economy deals with real needs," she says. "Real economy is the soil, the water, seeds, housing, the fiber of our clothes, the fuel for heating our homes."

It was this understanding that connected indigenous peoples to their land and gave them rich, abundant lives. There is no need for competition when the welfare of all, including the environment and all sentient beings, is considered of primary importance, Helena says.

"The people of the future will not be like the people of today, who only believe in logic and the reign of numbers and capital," Grandmother Bernadette says. "The future will go to those who have the understanding that the net worth of tomorrow's society resides in respect and consideration for the Other. With that understanding there can be no oppression."

Globally, we need to respect other people's ways, which requires exchanging arrogance for humility and ego for compassion, Carol Moseley Braun says. In helping people deal with oppression, she says, we must understand that the best we can do for ourselves, as well as those who are oppressed, is to help remove institutional barriers that keep them from making their own choices about their own lives. In helping people around the world have the ability to choose for themselves, to become educated, to have a chance to vote, to participate in their economy as they choose to, to raise their children in safety and care in a safe environment, we must not impose our own cultural values or make the egotistical assumption that we have it better than they do. That's just not necessarily true, she says.

"It is most important to begin by respecting the culture of others, respecting the Divine in each person and giving a person a chance to respect their own life," Carol says.

"We need to take all those qualities that have existed in most ancient cultures five thousand years ago," Gloria Steinem says, "and bring them into modern times."

We must also know that each of our voices is important in the struggle to fight oppression. Carol Moseley Braun tells a story to illustrate.

In the Tennessee legislature, there was a man named Henry Burn, who had voted against suffrage for women in the United States. Whether or not the vote happened in the rest of the country depended on what happened in Tennessee. The night before the crucial vote in Tennessee, Henry Burn received a letter from his mother, which said, "Vote for suffrage and don't keep them in doubt. Don't forget to be a good boy and help Mrs. Cat put the rat in ratification."

Henry Burn changed his vote the next day, to the surprise of everyone, and voted for the women's right to vote. His one vote made the difference. Tennessee's approval passed women's suffrage for the United States.

"We know about Henry Burn, his mother's letter, and his vote," Carol says. "But we will probably never know who spoke to his mother, what conversations she had, what inspired her to write that letter that changed her son's mind, changed his vote, and then changed the world. Each person's voice can make the difference in helping to convey a larger truth, helping to build community, and spreading a perspective about the world that will save it."

Gathering together in like-minded groups is important, Carol says. Others need to know there are people in the world who understand where their tears are coming from. "Rather than tears of pain, take that energy and find joy and light," she says, "because you are a force for the good in all of this."

Fighting oppression is a universal battle, Carol says, one that must be fought every day with every encounter. "The real question is, what are we going to do to serve and to combat the evil of oppression in our times? Are we going to turn away and pretend that it isn't there, or are we going to come together to build community, to engage to fight it *Oppression* worldwide, to fight it in our individual ways, in our individual places, but to fight it nevertheless?"

The more we reach outside ourselves to communicate our personal vision, our truth, and our understanding, the more likely we will be to touch a chord in the person listening, Carol says. The listener will be more motivated to respond in one way or the other. "All too often, people feel their views don't matter, that their voices aren't heard, so they keep their ideas to themselves and that doesn't help anyone. It is very important to communicate our truths, because we never know where that communication will take us, who will hear it and pass it along."

When we are a voice for the truth, we have weighed in on the right side of justice, Carol says. "Making a commitment to stand on the right side of the road is the only defense against people who have greed, anger, hatred, and violence in their hearts. Standing up can be an overwhelming task, but eventually, as more and more people join, their voices will add weight and change the imbalance."

The dark systems of capitalism and consumerism seek to exploit, suppress, and ultimately destroy life. Life on this planet is all about diversity, the Grandmothers say. We can no more change a mountain into an ocean, a forest into a desert, an elephant into a dog, or an orchid into a weed than we can change the ways we are all different. In this world, one culture is not better than another. Each represents a society's response to dealing with life. Different nations have different conceptions of things. We must not take it as wrong, as individuals or as nations, if another's ideas are not the same as ours.

Cultural diversity results from people's connection to the living world within their local community, Helena says. The ever-expanding scale of the global economy obscures the consequences of our actions, preventing us from acting with compassion and wisdom. We now operate from a very narrow view of human needs and motivations, and the selfishness in our nature is being exploited rather than tempered. We are losing touch with the world around us, and humanity is being eroded as a result.

"We need to be able to find a way to strengthen our voices, and the voice of life," Helena says. "We must pull ourselves out of the numbing trance and see that it is our man-made system of money and technology that is undermining all of us, vulnerable and strong alike. Technology is becoming our master, where it should be our servant. With life on a more human scale, there is less need for rigid regulations, and decision making can be more flexible. Less conformity is demanded. The further we are from the decision-making process, the more disempowered we feel."

Before all is lost, Helena says, we must return to our indigenous cultures to learn again how to live together. We must take our power back for our communities, our families, and ourselves. The global economy is not about interdependence, it is about being dependent on a few companies. Creating a global village assumes it is the chaotic diversity of cultural values that lies behind the conflicts of the past. If our differences are removed, then our differences will be resolved. But, instead, villages, rural communities, and their cultural traditions are being destroyed. Communities, like tribes, which have sustained themselves for hundreds of years, are disintegrating, and the spread of the consumer culture seems unstoppable.

"Erasing the differences between us does not increase harmony or promote understanding," Helena explains. "Intense competition for limited resources is what inflames ethnic and racial violence. Increasing poverty is suffocating life."

Her experience in Ladakh, as well as research in the West, has made it clear to Helena that "the rise in crime, violence, depression, even divorce, is to a very great extent a consequence of the breakdown of community."

In Ladakh, for instance, Helena has seen three-year-old children develop the stance that they are nobody if they don't have Levis or Nikes. "Basically, the children are begging for community, because they are being led to believe that this is how they will get the love from their peers. This is a very evil intervention into one of the deepest human needs, which is to be loved, to be part of community," Helena says. "Conversely, children growing up with a sense of their place on the

Earth and to others around them grow up with a sense of self-esteem and healthier identities and are less likely to oppress or exploit others as adults.

"So much destruction, disaster, and hatred stems from selfishness," Grandmother Tsering says. "Tibetans are brought up to daily think of another person's needs before our own. This way of thinking is the best training for the mind. Having a sound and clear mind is the most important factor in benefiting others. When we all put others first before self, we will finally achieve peace, harmony, and love. And we will naturally have compassion for ourselves."

We must fight for the voice of life, the Grandmothers say. But in fighting oppression, we must not get caught in the shadow of the same disease of oppression. Change must come, not with warlike measures, but with the strength of prayer. For example, the corruption in the Catholic Church that allowed for the passage of the doctrines of conquest had nothing to do with the seed teachings that are so vital to the church. We must address the place where disease and corruption were planted that have caused pain to so many people. It is really through prayer that we can begin to recover the seed of goodness in everyone.

"Peace is like a seed that you put into the Earth," Grandmother Maria Alice says. "If you take care of it, it will grow and give flowers. I believe that the children should water this seed a lot, and their caretakers must make certain the idea of peace is well planted in their hearts. The children, just as we all do, must believe that the world will bring something good for you."

We can let out the voice that is suppressed, Grandmother Maria Alice says, because the majority of humanity does not want war. They don't want what is going on in the world. "We don't need to wait for someone to give us freedom," she says, "because God gave us freedom. He gave us our lives, and we are here. We are alive. We are like Him."

Nature's Pharmacy

"THE FOREST IS LIFE," Grandmother Bernadette says. "The forest is our God-given pharmacy."

Traditional medical knowledge originates with plants, and therefore is as old as plant life on Earth, the Grandmothers say. Traditional knowledge is free and is received through prayer and offered in prayer, as prayer is the essential empowering element in traditional medicine. Every civilization has known traditional medicine. The knowledge of traditional medicine has been passed down through countless generations and thus has many lifetimes of testing and practice behind it. Modern medicine is actually founded upon traditional medicine, because the foundation for all medicine is plants.

In traditional medicine, illness can be understood as a communication from the spirit of a person, so in treating illness the medicine person works to understand what the spirit of the patient is calling for. Traditional medicine heals the body, heart, and mind, whereas modern medicine focuses on curing the body's ills. In traditional medicine, the whole person is addressed: his or her environment, relationships, mind, and spirit, as well as body. Traditional medicine also recognizes that the disease itself has a spirit as well: What does the disease need? Why did it come? What is it teaching the person? These are some of the questions traditional healers ask.

In the Mayan culture, medicine also includes philosophy, nutrition, and sacred sex, and its purpose is to help the patient realize the Divine within. The Mayans understand that a vacuum of love in a person's soul is created when sexual energies are out of balance. The person would suffer depression from a lack of soul caused by a lost connection to the sacredness of sex. Healing would come from a return to balance and to the knowledge of the ancestors.

Traditional healers around the world share the same secrets. These secrets come from nature and from an awareness of the integrity of all life and the interdependence of body, mind, and soul. Traditional medicines honor the four elements and the seven generations past and to come, knowing that as we heal, we are also healing our ancestors and future generations.

In traditional medicine the goal is to heal, whereas in modern medicine the goal is to cure, the Grandmothers say. Curing aims to make a disease go away, but the goal of healing is to return the patient to "wholeness" by restoring or enhancing harmony and well-being. A cure can often destabilize the rest of the system. For instance, taking an antibiotic can cure a specific infection but most likely will upset digestion or compromise the immune system, causing an infection in another part of the body or feelings of fatigue. Medication does nothing to empower patients in their healing process, and battling the side effects of strong medications like chemotherapy can be a lonely and difficult process.

Prayer and ceremony are an integral part of traditional healing methods and help patients feel a strong connection to their family or sources of support and also to a power greater than themselves. Healing renews patients' connection to nature and to themselves, sources of infinite strength. There is an understanding that a patient's healing can also bring well-being to the family and community. The patient actually has the opportunity to gain wisdom as well as health.

The measure of success in modern medicine is the cure, whereas healing in traditional medicine is the measure of a patient's well-being. Unfortunately, a cure can be measured scientifically, but the effects of healing cannot, because healing involves Spirit as much as science. In traditional medicine, a peaceful death can be considered a healing.

"It is so important to know that each sick person is a unique case," Grandmother Maria Alice says. "Traditional medicine is not like modern, where the same treatment is given to everybody. We heal in an integrated manner. Bodies may be sick in a similar way, but no two people

have the same spirit so no two people can be treated in the same way. *Nature's*
Even a mother and child do not have the same spirit." *Pharmacy*

That modern medicine deals with the disease much more than the health and well-being of a person is not a judgment, Maria Alice says. One is not good or bad. Good or bad is not the question, because both are part of the whole and part of a process. What is important is to try to understand both approaches.

Ten years or more of study are required to learn traditional medicine, as there are so many different types of plants. In addition, there are male plants and female plants, and they don't have the same virtues. Knowledge of the mind, emotions, and spirit is also required, because traditional medicine takes into account that there are three categories of illness: natural, psychosomatic, and spiritual. Although modern medicine deals with the first two, only traditional medicine deals with spiritual diseases or wounds of the soul.

All of these types of sicknesses are specific and are not treated in the same manner, Grandmother Bernadette explains. For natural sicknesses of the body like colds and teeth problems, there are specific plant medicines that are therapeutic. Sometimes nature can be the force behind an illness, as in the case of a snake bite. Illnesses like stress and insomnia, which are psychosomatic and come from what is happening in the mind, are the result of a certain way of life or a certain behavior and most often stem from society—for example, from being overworked or having financial problems. Spiritual sicknesses can be something a person is born with, she says, and are considered sicknesses of the soul.

When people have a spiritual sickness, they can suffer greatly, though the doctor may not see anything wrong, and an X-ray may not detect anything, Grandmother Bernadette explains. Nevertheless, the person is sick. Traditional medicine can heal in such situations. Every part of the world has what is known as a "master" or sacred plant that heals spiritual sickness. Peyote, Ayahuasca, Iboga, and the holy mushrooms of the Grandmothers' traditions are examples of the mystical plants that are used to heal spiritual sickness. In order for traditional medicines to heal the soul of a person, they have to be used in holy ceremony. Negativity is driven out through prayer and ritual.

Many plant remedies are known to all the people, so that a person can take care of themselves without consulting a physician. Other types of plants and trees are specific to certain, even very grave, illnesses. There are plant medicines for AIDS, alcoholism, cancer, skin diseases, anemia, diabetes—diseases that have all been healed by traditional medicine for many thousands of years. However, modern medicine doesn't want to allow traditional healers to be involved in healing the major illnesses, the Grandmothers say.

The Grandmothers discovered that they all have nearly the same traditional healing methods. Plants may be different because of the differences in climate and the land, but healing methods are similar. For example, purification is an important healing element in all their traditions, especially with sicknesses of the soul. Not only are plants used, but water and fire also are important methods of purification.

The environment in which a person heals is also considered very important. In modern medicine, people usually stay alone in their hospital rooms. But traditional healing methods take into account that when we are sick we need comfort, we need help, we need to be touched. In traditional medicine, a person is encircled and treated with affection to raise his or her morale and guard against feelings of isolation.

Yupik Grandmother Rita says that her people have used medicines from the land for thousands of years. Their healers know exactly what and how to treat with the plants and know all the side effects. But because they aren't scientifically approved, they can't use them.

Yupik healers also know that a thought can change the whole dynamic of the illness and the healing. For example, Grandmother Rita says, two patients can come in with the same kind of arthritis in the same place in the body, but it's not the same illness, because each person has different thoughts, and thoughts change things. "A thought is like lightning and can last only a half a second," she says. "Can you understand that through science? What science?"

In the healing process, Grandmother Rita says, we must begin with who we are, with the totality of our being. Our illness is often defined by our personal history. However, this personal history becomes fully

useful only once we are ready to accept the fact that we have created
our lives, and then let our past go.

In 1995, when doctors found cancer in her body, they told Grandmother Rita she was dying. Her family, children, and husband were crying, and she wondered if she should have surgery or just let go. "Something told me I had to keep living for today, for what was going to happen with the Grandmothers Council in the future. I wasn't ready to die, I guess. I had come into this world to do something."

Though she didn't know then how to pray, she prayed anyway, and everyone she knew was praying for her. "As I looked at all the flowers that had been sent to me, I said, 'These are my people. I can't leave them. Like the flowers, they had different faces, different smells, different shapes. Some were wilted, some were broken. I'm not going to leave.'"

So Grandmother Rita met with a friend and asked for permission to talk about all the ugly things that had happened in her life, and then she let them all go. The emotions we hold inside instead of expressing turn to disease, she says. We need to breathe feelings out instead of holding them in.

"We all have the power to redefine our past," Grandmother Rita says. "We must give ourselves permission to define ourselves beyond our history. It is important to acknowledge that we are alive and well, and that the past has taken us to a good place. The present is ours. Our past has brought us to the threshold of the present moment. With that understanding real healing begins."

In the Yupik tradition, all knowledge is gained by listening. "My elders used to tell us to put away the books," Grandmother Rita says. "We never hear stories only once. We hear them until they go into our whole body, so that it becomes a part of us. You listen and remember with your whole body, and the knowledge becomes a part of you, so that you don't have to go to a file. You can go into your own 'computer' and look for the file."

Grandmother Rita also "talks" with the plants, asking them to tell her how to use them for healing, and she has found that the information she gets is similar to the knowledge given to her by her elders. Because the Yupiks live in the tundra, most of their medicine comes from roots, although some comes from animal parts, particularly fish.

Stinging nettle is used for many things, but especially to prevent cancer and to clear the mind. Stinging nettle works on the serotonin levels of the brain. Grandmother Rita works primarily with people struggling with behavioral and mental health problems and uses stinging nettle for balancing her patients. She has also observed that Alzheimer's develops from becoming inactive as people grow older. Drinking a lot of water is very helpful with Alzheimer's, as it is for maintaining health in general, she says. It is extremely important to drink water to be clear spiritually, emotionally, and physically, she says. Combining stinging nettle with drinking a gallon of water a day can greatly alleviate the pain of arthritis. Stinging nettle can be put in soups and salads to help prevent cancer.

As in many other traditions around the world, the white birch tree is one of the most important sources for medicine in the Yupik tradition. In the Yupik language, the word for white birch means "strong," because white birch is recognized as essential for survival. White birch is used to make baskets, canoes, and drums. The leaves are eaten, and tea is made from the small seeds and used for colds and as a remedy for other ailments. The sap is used to make sugar—three or four buckets of sap make a large jar.

The Yupiks feel a spiritual connection with the white birch. "We are the birch," Grandmother Rita says. "When a tree falls, we are dying. But we know that the seeds will still grow and, when they do, we are the new seeds, the new leaves, the new branches. We are the roots."

The inner bark, or the membrane between the wood and the bark of the white birch, is used as medicine for cancer in the Yupik tradition. The inner bark is gathered two times a year: during the spring before the leaves come out and the sap is present, and in the fall after the sap goes back into the tree. The inner bark is dried and then pounded with a stone to make it into a powder. No machines are used. One-and-a-half level teaspoons of the powder are added to two quarts of water and boiled for three minutes, then left to cool and strained. One-third of a cup is taken three times a day for sixteen days in the treatment of cancer.

If another round is needed, the patient must wait ten days after the first treatment. The patient should stop the treatment after three rounds, according to Grandmother Rita. She says it is very powerful medicine and should never be taken without consulting a traditional medicine healer or a doctor.

Grandmother Rita planted traditional plants in a garden in front of the hospital in Anchorage where she works. The hospital won't let the medicines be used for healing, but the garden has become a focus of interest for the staff and patients nevertheless.

In the Grandmothers' traditions, mental illness is considered to come from a lack of harmony and balance. Any attempt to destroy life leads to imbalance. Equilibrium is restored through mental health or right thinking and spiritual influences. Grandmother Bernadette's tradition treats mental illness in a unique way. Instead of just calming the patient with tranquilizers, which in the end often just make people feel lethargic, traditional treatments, and not just medication, are used.

"When a person arrives, even if they are in chains, they are given a treatment, and they sleep all the way through the night," she explains. "While they are sleeping, a special kind of music that heals the mind is played. After another two months, we give them another treatment. We never put them off to the side as hopeless, and little by little the sickness disappears. The patient is healed. There are no secondary side effects. Our way of healing is natural, because we are using nature, so it helps humanity. This is important, because there are many, many cases of mental illness in the world today."

Medicine in Tibet was called the "Science of Nurturing," Grandmother Tsering explains. A great variety of medicinal herbs were harvested for healing. In addition, many different kinds of metals were used, including gold. One particular medicine was called the "Precious Pill," which took care of all cases of poisoning. Cancer was virtually nonexistent before the Chinese takeover, and Tibetans lived long lives. Now cancer is increasingly common. Since their occupation of Tibet, the Chinese are selling Tibetan medicine and marketing it with Chinese names.

Tibetan healing traditions are similar to traditional medicine practices around the world, with one great exception. Taming of the mind is an essential teaching in their Buddhist tradition, and because of their philosophy the people of Tibet were very happy, despite having no real wealth, Grandmother Tsering says. "If we all followed a true spiritual practice, the world would not all be in the situation it is in," she says.

Grandmother Flordemayo, whose mother was an herbalist as well as a midwife, advises people for the most part to concentrate on only a few plants that relate to their specific field of interest. For instance, the beautifully scented plant she is named after has multiple purposes. In addition to promoting lactation and shrinking the uterus, she says that it is currently being used experimentally in Mexico to retard AIDS. Even studying one plant, such as garlic, can be rewarding. Garlic is very magical, she says.

Spiritually and emotionally, the way to health is balance, Flordemayo believes. "But the road to understanding balance is an incredible road full of challenges, because everyone these days is going in different directions," she says. "My life has shown me that when we are out of balance, everything in our lives is thrown off. When we become an example of balance and inner peace, even just with our partner, children, friends, we are healing the planet, and we heal ourselves as well."

Illness is a communication from the spirit of that person. The medicine person works to understand what the spirit of the patient is calling for.

In addition, Flordemayo believes that our lives are predestined: we all have a time, a place, a mission. When we are aligned with our purpose, we are automatically in balance, and we aren't being taken in multiple directions. Even if we could bring that focus in for a split second every day, our lives would be better balanced. "Life is a mystery," she says, "and none of us have all the answers. All we can do is try."

In the Lakota tradition, you can't just go out and pick the medicines at any time. There were very real practical considerations. "If you pick a certain powerful root that is good for almost anything in the summer, then the snakes are going to be after you," Grandmother Rita Long Visitor Holy Dance explains. "Or the thunder and lightning beings will come down on you."

In the summer, when the plant is flowering, a stick is put in the ground to mark it until the wintertime, when the snakes won't come around and it will be safe to pick. "If someone is especially sick and needs the medicine in the summer, the medicine man has to go and pray to the root before he takes it out of the ground," Grandmother Rita explains. "As soon as he is done with it, he has to take it far away to where the trees are and hang it up. If the root is left in the house, the snakes will come."

There are many medicines for all the different sicknesses in the Lakota tradition. The membrane between the bark and wood of the Ponderosa pine is used for tuberculosis. Bear Medicine (medicine made from bear parts) is used for heart problems. These medicines, as in all traditional medicines of indigenous peoples, were discovered by observing the animals and by gaining information from the Spirit World or the plant directly through meditation and prayer. Many of the illnesses we have today have been healed by traditional medicines for thousands and thousands of years.

Fundamental to all healing is prayer, the Grandmothers say. "If you believe in God or the Creator with all your might, really put your whole mind into your prayers," Lakota Grandmother Rita says, "that is the thing that will help. If you pray one day and forget to the next, that won't help. If you are a believer in God, whatever church you belong to, your prayers can help you. You have to believe in your prayers, because God is the one who brought us here. He's the one taking care of us. He's the one who put us on that road. He's knows what you are going to be doing tomorrow and the next day. If you stay aligned with that, God will be with you."

Cheyenne Grandmother Margaret believes she is a testimony to indigenous medicine ceremony ways, the sacred ways of talking to the Creator that have healed so many for so long. Her son's interest in the ceremonies pulled Margaret back to them. "This is how the mystery works," she says. "I went back into the ceremonies saying, 'Oh, yes. Here's where I belong. My ancestors already put this healing path here for me.' I began sitting on Mother Earth, gathering all the pieces and tools of spirituality, and waking up."

It is a mystery how we are given seen and unseen guidance when we seek help for a problem. And it is a mystery how we are able to receive such guidance. When she was going through a difficult time trying to become sober, Grandmother Margaret saw a tree that was frozen and covered with ice. Looking at its beauty and understanding its symbolism in her life, she realized she had to learn to live by herself to stay sober, knowing her children were watching her. She realized she was a smart woman and needed to go back to school. Working with peyote in ceremony helped Margaret to heal from her past and her alcoholism and brought her back to her innate spirituality. Like her grandfather told her, the medicine has its own way.

Grandmothers Maria Alice and Clara drink the sacred medicine called Santo Daime. They live in a spiritual community that tries to practice what the holy medicine teaches.

"The holy medicine is in front of my path," Grandmother Maria Alice says. "The medicine has taught me a lot, opening my inner doors and windows to receive much more information about who I am, what I am doing here, and to clear my path in this world."

The information gained by taking the holy medicine is what brought Grandmother Maria Alice to live inside the forest and is showing her more and more about the mission she has in the Amazon and in the world. Her mission is to "gather all the different cultures and their traditional wisdom and to find a voice for all of us," she says. "One spiritual link that can express our gratitude to this forest that is our mother, our grandmother, our great-grandmother, that gives us health in our bodies and in our spirit and teaches us to be happy and trustful."

Of grave concern to the Grandmothers is creating a bridge between traditional and modern medicine, what they consider a very complex issue, given the vast difference in philosophies and approaches. The bridge between traditional and modern medicine must rely on the principle of equality, a dedication to the salvation of humanity, and a just exchange of resources.

"For us, such a bridge is not so complex," Grandmother Maria Alice says. "It is natural. We know we have the spirit. We have the fire, which is our eternal life. We have our bodies that are like travelers. For us, all plants, animals, and elements of nature are sacred. Each one has its own power, and some have special power when specially mixed. And those are mysteries that are inherited from our ancestors. We don't have ready remedies for standard illnesses."

Some spiritual medicines are more powerful, Grandmother Maria Alice says, and we need to deserve the healing from those medicines. Other medicines are not so powerful, but they help and support people in their process to reach the possibility of deserving and healing at deeper levels.

When a spiritual approach is taken toward an illness, even an insect bite that leads to malaria is an opportunity for a deeper spiritual awareness of the self. The illness becomes an opportunity for purification and a chance to learn more about our own spirit, our past, and transformations that are still needed. Illness can be an opportunity to learn who we are at the most profound levels, Grandmother Maria Alice explains, even to learn not to identify with our race or nationality or sex, but to know the meaning of "I Am," our true essence. Ultimately, she says, all of humanity is trying to remember that.

"We believe that God does not give us what we can't support," Grandmother Maria Alice says. "He always supports us with the challenge He gives us. We must remember that we are surrounded by God. He is in the water, the fire, the sun, the stars, the earth, the plants, the animals. We are God, so we can handle anything without fear and reach different states of awareness through our illness." Even healers are part of the process and can reach new levels of awareness with the patient, if they do their healing work with consciousness, she says.

Both traditional and modern medicine have much to contribute to each other, the Grandmothers say, but practitioners of both methods must think in a profound way about creating a bridge between the two. In opening the dialogue, the most important question to address first is whether or not both sides are sincerely and from their hearts interested in contributing to the health of humanity. If that is not the priority, then the dialogue is closed because the true motive is hidden, Grandmother Maria Alice says.

The Grandmothers are concerned that modern medicine approaches the dialogue from a place of power, that their truth is the main one, that it is the only legal way. Power is used economically and politically, and even through wars, to maintain this position. For example, some governments are currently trying to go after the people who use the holy medicine, Santo Daime. People from around the world are being put in jail for using the sacred drink. On the other hand, people who rely on traditional medicine, including those who use Santo Daime, believe that health is peace and health is equality. Divine power is given to us at our birth, Maria Alice says. We can approach each other from that natural place.

When entering a dialogue about traditional versus modern medicine, it is important to understand our differences, Grandmother Maria Alice says. When doctors of modern medicine are treating a disease, they will run many tests but most likely will not address the health of the patient, whereas traditional medicine practitioners will approach the patient from the point of view that the patient's health is going through a challenge. So the patient needs to support her earth or her fire or her water, her air or her spirit, her emotional body or her roots, which is another way of seeing a disease. If modern medicine could share the results of their studies into the cause and cure of disease, then traditional medicine could apply the research to the whole reality of the patient. In respecting each point of view and respective contribution, both approaches would be very helpful to each other. In fact, they can complement and complete one another, the Grandmothers say.

Legalization and money are of great importance. In many places around the world, traditional medicine is offered free of charge by anyone who claims to understand how it works. Traditional medicine needs to become regulated so that true practitioners can be distinguished from those who only claim to be practitioners.

Indigenous peoples are the guardians of the forest and the medicines, and are appointed by nature, the Grandmothers say. No one should be allowed to come in, take their knowledge, and transform it into commercial patents, with the possibility of a great deal of destruction to the forest and to the practice of traditional medicine and a lot of money going into only a few pockets. Such exploitation is a social sickness, they say. Great care must be taken to respect the forest and ensure its sustainability. Whatever is taken out of the forest must be done so in the spirit

of an equal and respectful exchange, and only after consultation with
indigenous peoples, the caretakers of the forest. But too often the old medicine people, walking libraries of traditional medicines, are conned by Western medical research companies into revealing their knowledge when they don't realize that these companies plan to take this knowledge and patent it for their own gain.

"They give them some whiskey and get them to reveal the plant secrets," Grandmother Bernadette says, "then return to the Occident and make millions. And the poor medicine man from Africa doesn't have a franc. We Grandmothers refuse to have this kind of exploitation continue."

The Grandmothers say that research on the healing properties of traditional plants belongs to the people. But justice needs to be on the table, so that all can share the benefits of this research, in both traditional and Western medical contexts. The material benefits that come out of the research need to go back to their original source, the indigenous peoples, for future work and to support the people who protect the forest.

In the Amazon, where there are a lot of riches, people are pitting tribes against each other, giving them arms to fight against each other, in order to take the wealth of the rain forest out of the country. "Money is being used to buy life, to force people who are suffering from material needs to sell their richness for nothing, for destruction," Grandmother Maria Alice says. "While we have riches, we have poverty as well. People don't have money. So they decide to no longer plant, because they are caught in the illusion of making money and becoming important in other ways. People are selling small animals and other things from nature for so little money. What is going on in the Amazon is very serious and very sad."

The desire of the Grandmothers is to save humanity. Because the plants help many people, they want them to be available and affordable to everyone who needs or wants them. "We ourselves have borrowed the knowledge from our ancestors, and we are the ones who need to pass the knowledge on to our children and the future generations," Grandmother Bernadette says.

"Humanity, all of us, have forgotten the power of the spirit of the sacred plants," Grandmother Flordemayo says. "We have plants on our planet for everything that ails us, but we are too busy to honor that."

Grandmother Flordemayo has a dream to help the children of the world learn to make a first-aid garden, so that they will honor and protect the sacred plants in the future. The garden would have plants that can heal scrapes, stomachaches, sprains, colds, flu, and fever, illnesses children are familiar with. Plants for preventative medicines and for cleansing would also be a part of the garden.

"When we become an example of balance and inner peace, even just with our partner, children, or friends, we are healing the planet."

Then, in a small way, the children can learn to be nurturers of the land and of the sacred seeds and to honor the spirit of the plants and the sacred waters. The body can then be honored as a temple of beauty.

Humans are not machines on whom we can experiment, Grandmother Bernadette says. We cannot play around with essential elements of nature. The desire to heal must come from the heart. To put money first as the reason to heal is wrong. Treatment of the sick person is the first consideration, not their payment plan. The Grandmothers condemn those who give money priority over the alleviation of suffering, who make money by keeping people ill. It's a form of abuse from the perspective of traditional medicine, which tries to prevent illness.

There are clinics in Thailand and elsewhere, where healers are using herbs, ritual, and prayer to heal AIDS and many other conditions, Luisah Teish says. "But the American Medical Association will not let those people speak here. In effect, the AMA allows people to die, so they can control profit. They need to lose power, so that the power can go to the healers."

To take the knowledge and practice medicine without taking the years required to understand the plants is making dirty money, the Grandmothers say. Healers in the Amazon have no interest in making patents of their medicine. "Patents were invented by those who are in competition," Maria Alice explains. "This is not part of our tradition. This knowledge does not belong to anyone. It belongs to all generations, past and future. We want the knowledge of our medicine to be written down and preserved but never patented. We have very sacred ways of preparing medicine, which is not by machines. Because our medicine always has a prayer inside, it heals on different levels."

The Grandmothers are also concerned with conserving the forest heritage. "We have destroyed so much to build buildings, to build homes," Grandmother Bernadette says. "It's wonderful to live in a nice house, but when you are sick, how are you going to get healed? The pharmacy of traditional medicine is the forest."

Traditional and modern medicine need each other, the Grandmothers say, and humanity needs for the two disciplines to work together. Practitioners of traditional medicine need to find a way to transform the plants into a form that is commercial in order to bring their benefits to the greatest number of people, and modern medicine can help. The Grandmothers know that there are many scientists who, like traditional medicine practitioners, love their work and want to heal humanity.

In Grandmother Maria Alice's community, there is what is called a Santa Casa—"Health House"—where people go when they are sick and also when they want to avoid becoming sick. Doctors and nurses from modern medicine collaborate with traditional healers and often go to the traditional healers for their own needs. Patients have the option of which medicine to use, modern or traditional. Sometimes they aren't ready to go deeper into the process of discovering the origin of their problem, and so prefer taking chemical medication to cure rather than heal.

Competition is a big obstacle to collaboration between modern and traditional medicines. If a patient is healed with one discipline, the other need not feel it lost something. "This kind of thinking would not be a good structure in our bridge building," Grandmother Maria Alice says. "A good structure for our bridge is surrendering one to the other."

Some doctors, who want to collaborate, have their hands tied by the law. If caught recommending traditional medicine to a patient, they can lose their license. Modern medicine slows down the process of collaboration by requiring its own research instead of trusting the thousands of years of research already done. In the Amazon, all spiritual knowledge and practice is free, but the sacred plants and accompanying prayers and rituals from this region, which are healing people from all over the world, are forbidden in most other countries.

Carol Moseley Braun experienced the effects of such discrimination against traditional medicine firsthand, when her doctors told her that she would have to have knee surgery. She returned to the Senate that day walking with a cane, and Robert Byrd objected to her cane, based on an old Senate rule dating back to Civil War times (when one senator was almost beaten to death by another with his cane). The rule was waived in this case.

After this incident, one of her fellow senators came up to her and said, "I'm the resident witch doctor. I'm giving you something that comes from trees and is native to my state. We can't get it marketed, because drug companies don't want it marketed, except for animals, for veterinary purposes. The FDA won't approve of its use on humans, but it is used underground."

The medicine enabled Carol to move about without a cane, but she still had a serious weakness in her knee and believed she still would need surgery. After being made ambassador to New Zealand, Carol visited a Samoan healer, and after three sessions no longer used a cane or any medications. She now lives in a four-story house, walks easily, and has no problem navigating the stairs.

After her experience, Carol believes the work of preserving what the planet has given us for our healing and to make us whole is of central importance. "The only way we can stay healthy and keep our planet healthy is to take care of these healing medications and remedies," she says. "They need to be preserved."

Prayer

ABOVE ALL, the Grandmothers are women of prayer. They pray from one heart that doesn't see differences among people.

"Prayer is the greatest thing I have as I walk upon this Earth," Grandmother Agnes says. "I am nothing without the Creator. When you have the Creator with you, you have the force behind you, and negativity doesn't take over you, even in the dreamtime. You can't change even your children except through prayer. Prayer is a duty that has been handed down from the Ancient Ones that went before us."

Grandmother Agnes has been called to pray all over the world. "It frightens me sometimes, when no words come," she says. "So I pray, 'Grandfather, give me the words. You know them. Please tell me what to say.' Then the words come. It overwhelms me when Spirit uses my voice. That's the human in me. With true prayer, the Creator gives the words. You don't need an education to receive them."

Prayer in indigenous traditions is seen as a communication with God/Creator/Great Spirit and/or the wise beings or powers that He created, and includes both listening and speaking. What is being sought is communion or unity with God, and an opportunity not only to express one's truth but also to listen to God's messages. Most often prayers are recited, chanted, or sung while standing in a proud, upright stance.

The Creator knows when you are really praying, Lakota Grandmother Rita Long Visitor Holy Dance says. So prayers must be said with great intention.

We must direct our prayers with much love and much light, Grandmother Clara says.

In the tradition of Nepalese Grandmother Aama Bombo, gods come in different forms according to their task. "We believe in thirty-three million gods and goddesses," she says. "We always pray to Mother Earth, Father Sky, the Sun god, and Moon god—all the spirits from around the world who support us. We are created by the Creator. He just takes many forms of the One. We are His creation. We drink the water, breathe the same air, so what we do with the air affects us all."

"To the people of the center (Central America)," Flordemayo explains, "the Grandmother is the one that brought all Creation into being."

One night when there was no moon and just the stars, Lakota Grandmother Rita prayed very hard, and now all her prayers have been answered, she says. "I prayed to see the Creator, and when I saw Him, he wasn't Lakota, He was universal." Grandmother Rita prays to the Creator all the time, even when she is cleaning house and cooking. She prays to keep the bad thoughts away. "Everything that is in this universe I pray about," she says. "The war, the weather, floods, hurricanes, volcanoes."

"Holy and sacred is prayer," says her sister, Grandmother Beatrice. "When someone prays, you pray along with them. We are all equal," she says. "When I listen to everyone's concerns, I sit with them and pray as they talk about what concerns them. I pray the Creator answers their prayers. Prayer is the main thing in my life. The only way to survive is through prayer. We can do many things, talk about many things, but if we don't have that prayer, we will never succeed."

Despite not being educated and not having any sort of degree, Grandmother Beatrice says that it is through prayer that she gets along in this world. Even though her life was often very hard growing up, still she always prayed. "The best thing I can say to anyone is pray, and the Creator will look down upon you and take care of you. He is the one that will. No one else can take care of us that way. It doesn't matter how much education we have or who we are, if we can't pray, the rest is nothing. The Creator is the one we have to tell everything to, the one we have to confide in, the one who will take care of us."

"The only way to survive is through prayer. We can do many things, talk about many things, but if we don't have that prayer, we will never succeed."

Grandmother Julieta says that we can ask the Creator to help us to listen to our inner voice. "The Creator is inside of us," she says. "We pray to the Creator for all of us, all of our sisters and brothers all around us, above us, under us. At this time, we need our faith. We need to make our beliefs stronger, so we can continue to do our spiritual work and continue helping others. We ask for our truth to grow stronger at this time. During these difficult times, we need to stay in prayer all the time."

We need to feel the pain of our people, Grandmother Agnes says, so that we can send that pain to our Creator through our prayers.

Taking on another's hurt and suffering, no matter what, builds compassion, says Grandmother Tsering. "Good things come from this attitude," she says. "You don't need church if you have this mental attitude. The good in the world comes from humanity."

We have to continually pray for our loved ones and our grandparents that went on before us, Grandmother Beatrice says. "They carried the prayer for us. It's our turn. We're carrying it for our families and for our grandchildren. That's where we are. We need to carry on like that."

Through prayer, Grandmother Beatrice's son, Aloysius, was guided to bring the peace pipe to Ground Zero in New York to pray for the people lost to 9/11, to release their spirits. Because the tragedy was so sudden, the spirits were confused and stayed there. Aloysius placed his peace pipe on the ground where the people died, filled his pipe and prayed, then placed sage on top of the pipe.

The Lakota people use the peace pipe to pray, and they use it in their Sun Dances. The pipe was given to them by White Buffalo Calf Woman, who showed them the right words and right gestures to use in prayer. She told them that the smoke rising from the bowl was Tunkashila's breath, the living breath of the great Grandfather Mystery. With the pipe, she told them, they would walk like a living prayer.

Aloysius and others, including his mother, went on to Washington, D.C., where they visited John F. Kennedy's grave. As Aloysius and Grandmother Beatrice walked up the hill, carrying their blankets and the peace pipe, people around them made way for them to pass.

"We climbed over the fence," Grandmother Beatrice says, "and Aloysius took his pipe and lit it from the eternal flame. He then took those spirits he had picked up from Ground Zero, made a prayer, and released them there."

When the Lakota pray, and especially when they are using the medicine wheel, they use their Indian name to speak to the Creator. When they are prayed for, they are prayed for using their Indian name. Their Indian name is the eternal name they are known by in the Spirit World and by the Creator. When children are given their Indian name, they are given a consecrated hairpiece made of feathers that they wear whenever they pray and during ceremonies.

In ancient times, many cultures around the world were given what is thought of as a divine blueprint for maintaining peace and harmony and which was used for praying, often called a medicine wheel. Repre-

"The prayers and teachings of the ancestors will light our way through an uncertain future."

sented in most medicine wheels are the four directions, the four basic elements, and the four races of man. Always at the center of the wheel is where the oneness of Creation is honored. Some medicine wheels are very elaborate, and some are simple. They are used in ceremonies with various intentions. The essential teachings of the medicine wheel are based on the belief that all people are born with spiritual values already given to them by the Creator, and the symbol is a way to awaken and remind people of their own inner wisdom.

"The Cheyenne have used the medicine wheel in ceremony since the beginning of time, when our Creator created us," explains Grandmother Margaret. "The principles in the medicine wheel are the pathway to balance and harmony within and without. The medicine wheel means relationship. It is a gate, the doorway to the spirituality of our life. This is how Spirit works. We use the medicine wheel in the Sun Dance ceremony, which is about life for us."

"The medicine wheel is very sacred to the Lakota people," Grandmother Beatrice explains. "At the center of our medicine wheel is a cross. The cross is humanity with arms outstretched, embracing all four races of the first people here on this Earth and representing the four corners of this Earth coming together in unity. The medicine wheel is the circle of life."

The circle is the universal symbol of wholeness, where the end is also the beginning, and represents the unity of all life, the Grandmothers say. Life is a circle that moves from birth to old age to death to new life. The circle is the most common shape in nature. When people sit in a circle, everyone is equal.

"The Lakota people know that we came from this Earth and we are going back to this Earth," Grandmother Beatrice says. "There is no way around it. We don't have to worry about when we are going to die or how we are going to die. It's up to the Creator. He put us here. He gave us a time to live here to do what we have to do. When that time is over, He calls us home. We're going to go home."

You have to respect the medicine wheel, Lakota Grandmother Rita says. "You don't hang it from the rearview mirror of the car. You don't leave it sitting just anyplace, especially if there is a feather in it. No matter what, the medicine wheel must be respected."

CEREMONY, ritual, vision quests, and plant medicines have been used for thousands of years by indigenous peoples to further enhance the imagination and to create doorways into the spiritual realms for a direct experience of God or for guidance. By tapping into their higher minds, they seek balance and purpose through the visions received. Experiencing expanded states of awareness, exploring the hidden recesses of one's own mind and the transcendent powers beyond it, need never be feared when done with the highest intentions, the Grandmothers say.

"All human beings are similar to the Creator," Grandmother Maria Alice says. "This is the biggest prophecy I have ever heard. So we are powerful. Our feelings are powerful. Our mind is powerful. We can do a lot of things."

There are many ways to pray, the Grandmothers say, and no right way. A prayer can be made in any moment we find ourselves. Their only advice is that people pray while filled with gratitude, and pray for all of Creation, since we are all a part of all Creation.

The Grandmothers believe that it will be the prayers and teachings of the ancestors that will light our way through an uncertain future. The following prayer was offered to the Grandmothers at their first gathering in October of 2004 by Grandmother Bernadette Rebienot:

Great Master of the Universe, we ask of You to listen to our prayers and to guard over Your children who are suffering and who are in misery. Everywhere the world cries. Man has lost all good sense. We have forgotten that we are brothers and sisters. We have offended Your laws.

Creator All Powerful, have pity on us. Dissipate the darkness and open the door to our hearts to the light of life, to the spiritual light.

In one voice, grandmothers from five continents have here united. We prostrate ourselves at Your feet, to all the life force of nature.

We implore Your indulgence. We have polluted nature, destroyed all the spaces You have created with love and peace. We beg You, teach us to love one another and to forgive, so that we may find love.

Spirits of the sun, of the moon, of the stars, of the seas, of the mountains, of the Earth, of forests, of air, of thunder, of water, of the spirit of fire, and of our ancestors—help us. Watch over our Earth, watch over our progeny. Awaken in our hearts tolerance and unity. Protect us from epidemics, from sickness, from natural catastrophes—signs of Your anger.

Thank You, Lord, for having protected us up to this day, and thank You for having brought us together. May Your sacred hand bless our work and may peace reign in the world. Glory to You.

Appendix
The Story Behind the First Gathering of
the Grandmothers Council

INDIGENOUS PEOPLE RELY ON ORAL TRADITIONS to convey the elements of their culture. The stories are important not just as information, but also as a container for understandings that are the basis for going forward in life. As such, it is critical that the stories be told in their entirety, with nothing left out and nothing changed. Such is the story you are about to hear: the story of the vision that invoked the Grand mothers Council.

Though the Grandmothers Council had been seen in many visions and been foretold for hundreds of years, it was the vision of a sacred basket seen by Jyoti (Jeneane Prevatt, PhD) that set the prophecy in motion. At the time of her vision, Jyoti was not aware of the pre-existing prophecy about a Grandmothers Council. Jyoti's vision was a response to constant prayers to find a way to preserve and apply the teachings of the original people.

Three years after the creation of Kayumari—Jyoti's spiritual community in California—a woman, whom Jyoti called "Our Lady" appeared to Jyoti in a vision and presented the community with a mission. Our Lady said, "I am going to hand you my basket. In it are some of my most precious jewels. They are lines of prayer that go back to the original times. You are not to mix them or change them. You are to protect them and keep them safe. Bring them through the doorway of the millennia and hand them back to me, for I have something I am going to do."

As time passed, many in the community began to hear an inner prompting, "When the Grandmothers speak." At first, they didn't know what that could mean, but they began to receive inspiration about invoking a gathering of women. They began to hear prophecies saying, "When the Grandmothers speak, the door to unity will open to us all."

Soon after, Jyoti traveled to Gabon, Africa, with her children and a dear friend, Ann Rosencranz. They went to speak to the Bwiti elder, Bernadette Rebienot, about a plant medicine that helps tame the beasts of addiction. Some Westerners had been taking these plants out of the forest without asking the people of the forest, so they went to ask for her permission. During their visit, Ann and Jyoti were prompted to ask Bernadette what she thought about the idea of forming a grandmothers' council. She became quite animated and exclaimed, "Yes, it is time. It is time to bring the grandmothers together now. You must put this into motion."

Bernadette then showed Jyoti a letter she had just signed, along with Peruvian shamans who worked with the medicine plant ayahuasca. The letter created a motion of solidarity claiming their rights as indigenous people to be guardians of the planet.

Feeling a sense of urgency after their visit, Jyoti traveled to South America to see friends and family. During her visit with Marie Alice Campos Freire, she spoke of the letter Bernadette had signed. To Jyoti's astonishment, Marie Alice brought out an almost identical letter to Bernadette's, that she had just signed with six tribes of the Jura area of the Amazon. That was when Jyoti knew it was time to bring the Grandmothers together.

Overwhelmed by the scale of the vision, and uncertain of her ability to bring it about, she again prayed for direction. How was she to find the Grandmothers, and how would she know if she had the right ones? The answer came: "At the seed of all things are relations. Start there and everything else will grow."

Following the guidance of her vision, she turned to contacts she and members of Kayumari had already established through years of visiting and learning from indigenous peoples around the globe. Finally, Jyoti sent out letters of invitation to sixteen women elders. Thirteen accepted. All the Grandmothers who accepted said they knew deep within that they were meant to participate. They knew the Grandmothers from the Spirit World, the wise ones humanity has forgotten, were calling them to action.

For more information on the continuing events and activities of the International Council of the Thirteen Indigenous Grandmothers please contact:

The Center for Sacred Studies
P.O. Box 745
Sonora, CA 95370
(209) 532-9048
Jyoti, Spiritual Director
Carole Hart, Media Director
Ann Rosencranz, Program Director
info@grandmotherscouncil.com
www.grandmotherscouncil.com
www.sacredstudies.org
www.forthenext7generations.com